The Vasectomy Doctor

The Vasectomy Doctor

a memoir

DR ANDREW RYNNE

MERCIER PRESS

MERCIER PRESS
Douglas Village, Cork
Email: books@mercierpress.ie
Website: www.mercierpress.ie

Trade enquiries to CMD Distribution
55A Spruce Avenue, Stillorgan Industrial Park
Blackrock, County Dublin
Tel: (01) 294 2560; Fax: (01) 294 2564
E-mail: cmd@columba.ie

ISBN 185635 483 0
10 9 8 7 6 5 4 3 2 1

A CIP record for this title is available
from the British Library

 Mercier Press receives financial assistance from
the Arts Council/An Chomhairle Ealaíon

Printed and Bound by J. H. Haynes & Co. Ltd, Sparkford

Contents

Acknowledgements

First of all I should thank my editor at Mercier Press, Mary Feehan, for her courage and conviction in running with this effort of mine. Then my wife, Joan, for her forbearance and patience with me throughout – living with a writer is not easy. Thanks to my friend, Victor Egan, whose idea it was in the very first instance that I write this book. Thanks too to my old friend, Ronnie Drew, for writing such an honest foreword, and to another old friend, Dick Warner, who agreed to launch the book for me. I need to thank Joan Mulroy, my secretary of more years that either of us care to admit, for going through the book correcting the hundreds of misspellings that I managed to make and that the word-processor lets through. Another friend who needs to be acknowledged is Bryan Fox who was, as always, generous with his sound legal advice. Finally there are my son, Lorcan, and daughter, Caoilfhionn, who hovered in the background and worried for their mother's sensitivities. I hope those worries have proved groundless.

Dr Andrew Rynne
http://www.vasectomy-ireland.com

Foreword

Storytelling is, I have no doubt, an activity which is practised and enjoyed to a greater or lesser degree throughout the world. In Ireland it seems to be a national pastime and I can assure you, from my personal experience, that everybody in Ireland has stories to relate. On most days if you're out there knocking around you can encounter at least some people either telling or aching to tell their tales. Over a period of many years I have listened to and enjoyed all sorts of stories, some great, some good, some bad and some that were really awful, but overall I have been greatly enriched by the experience. I look forward to being further enriched by reading Andy's memoir.

I have known him for many years. I can't remember exactly when we met; it must have been sometime in the early 1960s, but you must take into account that there was a lot of euphoria 'flowing' around that time. This was a period when Irish music and song was being celebrated in Dublin. While there was in England and America what was called the 'Folk Revival', what was happening in Ireland was what I suppose could be termed a resurgence. Traditional music had never died out and even in Dublin there were two traditional music clubs, the 'Pipers Club' in Thomas Street, and another in Church Street, which had an official name but I can't remember what it was, we jackeens called it the 'Fiddlers Club', a name which may have appeared very irreverent to some of its members.

In other places like the 'Coffee Kitchen' in Molesworth Street, 'O'Donoghues' pub in Merrion Row and many places besides, Irish music was being played and Irish songs were being sung, along with songs from many other parts of the world. Luke Kelly had just returned from England and brought with him many songs we had not heard before, songs written by Ewan McColl which in many cases carried a strong social comment. Johnny Moynihan could be heard singing songs from all corners of Ireland. Songs of Dublin were being unearthed by people like Frank Harte and others, all greatly helped by Colm O'Lochlainn's books of 'Street Ballads'.

There was a great excitement in the air at that time with new people constantly arriving at the various venues to sing and exchange songs; it was not an elitist circle by any means, all were very welcome.

Andy Rynne was a part of all this and was respected as a fine singer and whistle player. I still enjoy his company when we meet at parties and other get-togethers. He, for his part, maintains his enthusiasm and willingness to perform at the drop of a hat. Andy Rynne who, because of his integrity, and his ability to pay attention, observe and to take note of the many interesting incidents, nuances and experiences within his own life and in those lives being lived around him, is well qualified to tell his story or present his memoir.

Well done Andy.

Ronnie Drew
August 2005

To my wife Joan

CHAPTER 1

Point Blank Range

Thursday afternoon, 12 July 1990, was no different from most others. I was working my way through a short list of vasectomies and seeing a few general practice patients in between. My secretary, Joan Mulroy, was sitting at the reception desk outside in the waiting-room. I had just given my patient a local anaesthetic into the side of his scrotum and around his *vas deferens* on both sides. So far so good. Vasectomy is a tricky operation requiring maximum concentration. This was my twenty-something thousandth vasectomy and I quipped with my client that I was getting the hang of doing them and that I had it all down to a fine art. This doctor–patient banter has evolved over the years and is designed specifically for vasectomies to put the man at ease. Some doctors refer to this as 'talk anaesthetic' and it is of the utmost importance. After all, the area being operated on is one that all men instinctively protect with their hands as they walk across a pitch-dark room for fear that they may bump into the sofa. And now it is being laid bare and ever so gently and skilfully assaulted with syringe and fine needle, scalpel and forceps. I have the greatest admiration and respect for the courage and trust of all men who present themselves for vasectomy. A quiet babble of reassurance is essential. In addition to this, nowadays a large flat screen hangs from the ceiling above the patient's head onto which beautiful images of Irish scenery, rivers and streams, forests and mountains are projected from a DVD player. But in 1990 flat screens and DVDs were yet to be invented.

An upsetting noise was coming from the waiting-room up the corridor, but I wasn't too alarmed. I thought it might have been a child getting sick and maybe being rushed to the toilet down the hall or something like that. This kind of thing happens all the time in general practice. But the kerfuffle was no sick child. Within seconds and without any warning the door behind me bursts open. By the time I swing around to see what is happening the barrel of a .22 rifle is coming into the room, quickly followed by a short dark man with his right index finger on the trigger and the stock of the gun held firmly to his right shoulder. He is wearing a black woolly pudding-bowl hat and black gloves. The trigger guard has been taken off the gun and the gun is pointing directly at my head. The gun has a magazine clipped in place but at this stage I cannot say if it is loaded or not. This cannot be happening, this cannot be for real. Is this some kind of bizarre kissogram or something? Is this someone's idea of a joke?

But it is no kissogram and it certainly is no joke. This is deadly serious and my little surgery is suddenly filled with a lethal air of menace. I am getting a hideous sense of finality here. Time seems to stop. The gunman moves around to my right. He never takes his meaty finger off the trigger nor does he ever stop bearing down the sights straight at my head. I get the impression that he has been practising this at home. The patient for vasectomy, whose scrotum and its contents I had only a minute beforehand anaesthetised, gets off the operating table, pulls his pants back on and leaves the room quickly. I am now alone with my tormentor. He mutters something incoherent like: 'You ruined my life eight years ago so I am going to take yours now.' Then he comes straight at me and holds the muzzle of his rifle two inches away from my lower forehead, straight between my eyes. Now I am looking directly down the barrel and I can see the rifling or screw worm its way back into the gun. The barrel moves ever so slightly with his breathing. Otherwise he is rock steady and holds the gun in that position for what seems to me to be an eternity.

That screwing grove going back down the barrel is designed to make the bullet spin as it charges its way from breech to muzzle. By the time the bullet leaves the rifle it will be spinning like a dentist's drill at 1,000 revolutions per second. Spinning like that it will leave the muzzle at about 1,200 feet per second or 800 miles per hour – faster than the speed of sound. All the meaty finger inside the glove has to do now is exert five pounds of pressure on the trigger. This may sound like a lot but in fact it is nothing. A gloved finger does not properly sense how much pressure it is exerting on the trigger. I have misfired guns through the use of gloves more often than I care to admit. The situation I am now in is lethally precarious. Death will only come nearer once more in my lifetime and that is when it will take me off with it. Old meaty finger here could easily make a mistake. But whether by mistake or by design it hardly matters. The entrance wound between my eyes would be neat, tiny and bloodless. The exit wound at the back of my head would be hen's egg-sized and hideous.

Then slowly the gunman drops his rifle away from my face and directs it onto my lower abdomen. Now I have the impression that perhaps he does not intend to kill me. This is an impression that I may have to review in a few minutes' time but just at this very moment I feel a fraction safer than I did seconds before. Now I try to push him away from me but somehow the instrument trolley comes between us and goes crashing to the floor. There are vasectomy instruments all over the place. Two vasectomy forceps, a haemostat, a scalpel handle with a number fifteen carbon steel surgical blade attached, a five cc syringe loaded with two per cent Xylocaine, surgical swabs and a galley pot filled with Hibitane. All these things are now scattered across the floor.

Before I try to take him on again he pulls the trigger and the room is filled by a loud bang. He brings the bolt backwards and the empty shell flies out. He shoves the bolt forward again and locks it down. I felt nothing at all but there is blood running down the front of my right trouser leg. I have been hit, but exactly where I cannot say. Had it not been for all the blood and the loud crack of the rifle I would not have known that I had been shot. I say to my attacker: 'You've shot me, you bastard' and then I fall to the ground. He is over me still pointing the gun directly at my face. Now of course I know that the gun is loaded and this whole thing has taken on a more deathly dimension than ever.

Suddenly I get up off the floor and am amazed to find that I have two good legs under me. So why did I fall? I do not know but it hardly matters. What matters now is that I have both legs under me and I had better start using them to good effect. I make a bolt for the door and am away up the corridor. As I reach the empty waiting-room there is a second bang as the gunman fires at me again. Since I felt nothing as the first bullet entered the top of my leg I could not know now if he has hit me again or not with his second shot. Being shot is a painless business. I hear myself roaring. I do not want to roar like this but it seems to me that my body has gone into autopilot and is doing things of its own accord. Outside a patient is coming in to see me. I grab her by the wrist and try to pull her along with me and tell her what's going on and that there is a gunman in there with deadly intent. She falls to the ground and I stop to help her and the gunman is outside the surgery and barely ten feet away from us.

Next an extraordinary thing happens. The man who nearly had a vasectomy, his trousers by now safely back on, walks up to the gun-man and offers him a cigarette. The gunman accepts the cigarette and lights up. The man who nearly had a vasectomy is only trying to calm the situation down and to this day I am grateful to this man who I never met since. Now, for the second time I get the incorrect impression that the worst of the attack is over. It is not. With the cigarette sticking out of the corner of his mouth the gunman slides the bolt of his rifle forwards and backwards once again. I can see the empty shell arch its way to the ground glittering in the summer sunlight as it makes its way. Again the gunman lifts the rifle to his shoulder and fires right at my head. I know he has fired straight at my head because once again I am treated to a view directly down the barrel of his rifle. The tip of a branch of a leylandii bush parts company with the hedge one inch away from my left ear. It is time to get going again.

As I run up the short driveway towards the street there is another bang. This is his fourth shot at me and the third time that he has missed. I take a sharp left and left again. Now I am running diagonally across an empty space at the back of St Ann's where I once lived. He is after me and still shooting at me. I take a leaf out of the snipe's flying manual and start running in a zigzag fashion making myself a difficult moving target for a rifleman. Soon I am out onto the main street of Clane and running in front of St Ann's and around to the back of the house were I find my colleague Xavier Flanagan loading his golf clubs into the back of his car. Xavier wants to know what's wrong with me because I look dreadful. When I tell him that I've been shot he finds it difficult to believe. But then he sees all the blood down my right trouser leg and has to agree with my self-diagnosis. At this stage I am absolutely knackered and need to sit down. Xavier props me up on a garden chair on the raised patio at the back of his house and the thought occurs to me that the gunman could round the corner at any second and there I'd be cocked up on a chair, a grand target for even a mediocre shot like old meaty fingers.

What has happened in the meantime is that my attacker, unbeknownst to me of course, has taken himself into a field across from my surgery and threatened to shoot himself and anyone else who comes near him. About forty-five minutes after I have been shot Xavier lays me out in his car to drive me up to Clane Hospital. As we are passing the field where my attacker is I can see him out in the middle of the field sitting on the grass with the rifle across his knees surrounded by cattle. By this stage an enormous crowd has gathered and are viewing proceedings from whatever vantage point they can find. The army arrives complete with tear-gas canisters and the whole place takes on the appearance of a small battlefield.

The x-rays at the hospital show that the bullet has lodged in my right hip joint and I will need surgery to get it out. All things considered my kind colleagues advise that I go to a bigger hospital to have the job done and I agree. I may have founded Clane Hospital but that does not mean that I was unaware of its limitations at the time. At midnight I was put to sleep in St James' Hospital in Dublin and three hours later orthopaedic surgeon Garry Fenelon dislocates my hip joint and, with considerable difficulty, manages to get the bullet out. It now sits in a plastic envelope on the dresser at home here in the kitchen. I recover quickly. In four days' time I am back in Clane Hospital for a few days respite before getting the stitches taken out. While there my friends Dick and Geraldine Warner send me in a pint of Guinness covered with cellophane. Seldom has a pint tasted so good. Another old friend of mine, Paddy McKenzie, sends me in a vintage Châteaux Margot; that also is a memorable experience.

* * *

My surgeon advised that on no account was I to go to Scotland for grouse shooting that year. In Scotland the grouse-shooting season opens on 12 August, the so-called 'Glorious Twelfth', and that was just one month after having my right hip dislocated to extract the bullet. But I felt fine and decided to ignore the good doctor's advice and go to Angus anyway for our annual two days of walked-up grouse shooting on the heather-clad mountains over Balintore Castle. I'd been going there for years and I was damned if I was going to let recent happenings interrupt such a fine tradition.

Grouse are a fast flying bird slightly smaller that a hen pheasant and are native to the upland areas of Scotland and Ireland. Their staple diet is shoots of young heather, and to help them survive in good numbers it is necessary to burn off the heather in large patches to encourage new growth. But they also need older heather to provide them with shelter against the winds and the rains. We have very few native Irish grouse now in Ireland because nobody manages the moors where they might otherwise flourish. In Scotland on the other hand grouse-shooting is looked upon as a significant industry and all grouse moors are accordingly carefully keepered and managed.

If you know about these things one glance at an upland grouse moor in Scotland will tell you to which estate it belongs. Each keeper has his own way of burning off heather in a pattern that is unique to him alone. Thus all these low, smooth mountains are tattooed with the heather burn marks characteristic of that shooting estate.

The guns are arranged in a straight line across the moor and the dog-handlers follow some twenty yards behind. Every now and then the guns come onto a covey of grouse hidden in the long heather. A covey is a family or clutch of birds containing two adult parents and anything up to twelve mature offspring. They might all take to the air in one great flurry of activity or, more usually, they may get up in smaller groups of two and three. Once a bird has been shot down a whistle is blown and the line of guns stops moving forward. The dog-handlers unleash their retrievers and they go forward to try and retrieve the shot grouse. This sometimes can take ten or even fifteen minutes to achieve because at that time of year with all the heather pollen blowing around the place scent is poor and dead birds hard to pick up. But the code of practice whereby every shot bird must be picked up is not one lightly dismissed and it is a matter of honour that nothing gets left for a fox unless it is absolutely unavoidable.

I can sit on the dry heather while waiting for all birds to be picked up, take a breather and talk to my neighbouring gun or to a Scottish dog-handler or bird carrier. But if I wish I might just want to be left to my thoughts and be allowed to take in the spectacular views that upland grouse moors always and unfailingly afford. While so musing this may be a time to take stock and wonder exactly why I was shot one month ago and if there was any way of ensuring that this will not happen again and was I not incredibly lucky to have escaped with my life and what a great life it is too. Reflective moments like this are important.

CHAPTER 2

Third World Ireland

The postman came on foot. He had a limp, something to do with having been kicked by a cow. He didn't have a bicycle and of course he didn't have a car, only doctors and priests drove cars in those days. He walked. We called him Joe the Post; his full name was Joe Devine. He did more than just bring the post up to the house from Healy's post office down in Prosperous each day. He was also our eyes and ears, our lifeline to the outside world beyond the tall beech trees, the limes and sycamores and avenue's end. Television was yet to be invented and we had no radio, no phone, no transport other than Judy the pony and her trap. And no electricity. The Post would know who was dead and who was dying. More cheerfully, he would know who was born and who was getting married, who was making hay or who was cutting turf. This wasn't idle gossip either I'd have you know. These snippets of information were vital if you had hay down or were wondering where you might buy some decent firing come the autumn. He could forecast the weather for you as well.

'What's the weather going to be like this afternoon, Joe?' my father would want to know. Joe the Post would then make a careful survey of the summer skies and with a freshly sucked finger held aloft he would check the wind's direction and speed, for this was a serious business requiring skill and consideration.

'I'd say you would get the odd light shower this afternoon, Boss.'

That afternoon there would be an odd light shower. In this way Joe the Post was a walking almanac, a meteorologist, a newsman and reporter, a soothsayer and a wise man. He also brought around letters and parcels in an old canvas bag with a leather strap round his shoulders.

The Second World War is coming to an end. Dreadful, cruel, inhuman and hideous things have happened and are still happening. But I am oblivious to them all. It is 1945 and I have just passed my third birthday. The ration books are out and Joe the Post tells us that there is a big pile of turf up in the Phoenix Park. When the Post leaves it is my job to distribute the letters around the house. I can't read of course but Janie Ennis in the kitchen tells me that these are for the study and these for the schoolroom upstairs. First port of call then is the study where my parents, Stephen Rynne and Alice Curtayne, are seated across from each other at a large partner's desk. The room is a cube, eighteen feet long, eighteen feet wide and eighteen feet high. Each has a Remington Rand typewriter in front of them and the place is alive with the clack-clack of keys on paper and the ring of the little bell three letters before the end of the line prompting the writer to return the carriage and start a new line. My father uses two fingers only while my mother flies along in a properly trained manner. The room smells of Sweet Afton smoke and buddleia. My father reading aloud the last paragraph he has written occasionally disturbs the clack-clack of the typewriters. This you might think was a rather eccentric way of writing but then eccentricity and my father were no strangers.

The next lot are to be taken upstairs to the schoolroom. Here the governess, Kathleen McGowan, from Grange, county Sligo, holds sway. She is teaching my older siblings, Bridget, Catherine and Davoc, the rudiments of reading, writing and mathematics. I am excluded from this institute of higher education on the basis of my tender years and am relegated to the role of office boy bringing the post around the house. But my turn will come.

There was a lot of religion around at the time and our house – Downings House, just outside Prosperous in county Kildare – was no different from any others in this respect. Grace before and after meals and bedtime prayers were standard fare. A picture of Madonna and Child hung in the big hall downstairs and others of

Dante, St Paul, and The Last Supper hung upstairs in the landing. There was never a Sacred Heart for some reason. I expect that my parents thought it in bad taste. Even at three years of age I at least had a sense about the devil and angels, heaven and hell, sin and sanctifying grace.

I was sleeping one night upstairs with Miss McGowan. ('Miss McGowan, the head of the town, one leg up and one leg down' we used to sing at her.) I must have told a lie or something that day because I remember the devil was under my bed and he came out and bit me in the right elbow. The devil then spirits himself across the nursery floor and goes down the wash hand basin. I lie closer to Miss McGowan. I am three years old and it's one of my very first memories – the devil biting me in the elbow. God help us.

The winter of early 1947 has to go down in the annals as one of the worst winters in Ireland for a few hundred years. The *Monthly Weather Bulletin* of March 1997 describes it like this:

Early 1947 was very wet and stormy with flooding in many places, but it was not until 24 January that the spell of severe cold weather began. By the beginning of February there were already reports of skating on frozen ponds and the unrelenting cold continued until the middle of March. The temperature did not rise above 5 degrees C at Dublin airport between 22 January and 7 March and on most days during this period the temperature struggled to rise above freezing. In addition, a harsh easterly wind persisted for several weeks as the normal run of Atlantic depressions were diverted to the south of the country. There were between 20 and 30 days with snowfall in most places during this time and snow lay on the ground at Dublin's Phoenix Park for all but two days between 26 January and 8 March. Even at Valentia Observatory, where there would normally be snow on around 4 days during the first three months of the year, snowfall was recorded for a total of 50 hours over 14 days during the cold spell.

Indeed I can vouch for all of that. Our neighbour, Tom Dunn, husband of Madam Dunn, the piano teacher from Firmount, called in one day during March 1947 to discuss with my father the absolutely dreadful weather conditions and how they were making farming all but impossible. I was ear-wigging on their conversation, though of course I may as well not have been there at all as far as the two men were concerned. Tom described a scene at his farm that has stuck with me all my life. He said that his cattle were so hungry that one bullock actually got his front legs onto the trunk of a tree in order to be better able to eat a clump of ivy that was growing beyond cattle reach. You would need to understand just how stupid cattle usually are to fully appreciate how extraordinary a story this is. For a bullock to be able to figure out this kind of ingenious way to a square meal says a great deal about the extent of his hunger and the foul weather conditions of the time.

Speaking of Madam Dunn, the music teacher, reminds me of the first great fright that I ever got in life. Piano teachers, as indeed pianos themselves, were a bit thin on the ground in rural Ireland in the mid-1940s. People had quite enough to be doing trying to keep body and soul together without thinking about pianos or how to play them. But for some reason my two older sisters, Bridget and Catherine, and my older brother, Davoc, were all packed off for piano lessons. I was excluded from these on the grounds of being too young. Madam Dunn, two miles up the road and across from the Firmount TB sanatorium, was as we might say these days, the business. I would be left sitting outside on the steps of the old Victorian pile while my siblings were being put through their finger exercises in this academy of music inside.

Some sounds stay with you for all of your life and to this day I can still remember the sound emanating through the open window of Madam Dunn's parlour and my brother and two sisters inside getting their piano lessons. Even to the ear of a five-year-old child as I was then, that piano was so out of tune that, were it not so painful to listen to, it would actually have been quite funny. I would safely say that the thing had not been in tune since around the time of the Crimea. Hideous were its notes, repugnant its tones. Is it any wonder that none of us went on to become concert pianists with such a distorted introduction to the instrument? Any similarity between the sounds emanating from this instrument of torture and those one might hear coming from a proper piano in tune were purely coincidental.

Once, having had quite enough of listening to this cat's concert wafting out through the open window of Madam Dunn's parlour, I wandered off to the farm yard for some light relief. This was a bad mistake. In the yard I discovered a flock of very large bronze turkeys, all hens except for one cock. The cock spotted me of course and took an instant dislike to my presence amongst his precious hens. When a gander goes to chase you he holds his neck straight out in front of himself and his head is positioned one inch above the ground. This he swings to and fro in a menacing arch all the while making a silly hissing sound. But when a turkey cock goes into attack mode he does the very opposite, he holds his head back in the ready-to-attack-you position and remains silent. The turkey cock might be marginally more intelligent than the gander but there wouldn't be a lot in it.

Anyway this old turkey goes into his attack routine and with all those old dangly yokes hanging from his forehead he goes bright red in the face and takes off in my general direction. Sensible adults in this situation would stand their ground. But to me, a then five-year-old child, such an option seemed somehow very unattractive. I turned on my heels and ran for dear life with my tormentor in hot pursuit, his open beak within striking distance of my arse. As I fled past the open window from where a minute earlier ghastly sounds had been emanating, my terror and overall discomfiture were very little relieved to discover that the musicians and their maestro were on a short break and were all standing at the window being greatly entertained by the chase going on outside.

In or around the same time that Tom Dunn's cattle were climbing the trees trying to find a bit of sustenance for themselves, I am taken on the trip of a lifetime. Not far from Downings House runs the Grand Canal making its lazy way from Sallins past Soldiers Island and on to cross the Liffey via a triumph of eighteenth-century engineering that we call the aquaduct. That considerable feat accomplished, the Grand Canal then mooches along to cross under Digby's bridge and on past the tall beeches of Landenstown where Englishmen and Dubliners sit all day under enormous green umbrellas watching their floats and fishing for bream, tench, perch and roach, baiting them with live maggots.

On the opposite bank stands a great heron also fishing. I have always thought of the heron as a forlorn and doleful wading bird but I suppose if we had to stand up to our knees in water all day, hoping that some kind of meal would present itself, we too would have to be forgiven for a certain dolefulness. It must be akin to being in a very bad restaurant where the waiter is drunk and you are wondering will he ever bring out a starter or a main course. Or will you be fed at all? The heron's life is a precarious one. He holds his dagger-like beak poised just above the water's surface ready to strike at whatever comes by and presents itself.

From here the canal swings left at Tom Garry's lock and down through a straight narrow gorge heavily overhung from each side by ancient hawthorns, hazel, blackthorn, briars, alder and ash. Now the canal slips in quietly under the twisting Cock bridge, so called because there once was an alehouse adjacent to this bridge called The Cock. From here the Grand Canal turns in a more westerly direction and heads on out through a canyon cut deep into a raised sand quarry where we pick sloes in the wintertime to make sloe gin as a pick-me-up for when we will be out on the bogs snipe-shooting later in the year. From here the Grand Canal then goes in under Healy's bridge, locally pronounced Hayle's bridge, though in fact it's Bonynge bridge according to the plaque on its side dated 1784. At this point the canal gathers itself nervously and readies itself for its final assault down to Robertstown with the hill of Moods to its right and the bad lands of Mylerstown to its left. Finally then it pulls up outside the door of the first Grand Canal Company Hotel where 200 years ago weary horse-barge passengers once dined on Kildare mutton, syllabub and port wine.

This dreadful year and terrible times of February and March

1947 when livestock were climbing the trees, the Grand Canal, usually majestic and useful, has to suffer the rare indignity of being frozen solid and rendered useless. But my father Stephen Rynne, ever inventive and always eccentric, found a use for it. He took his bicycle down to Healy's bridge where there is easy access to the canal surface itself. Here he launches himself off in the general direction of the Cock bridge with me, two months away from my fifth birthday, on the carrier behind. And we're whizzing along at a rate of knots. This is cool, this is mighty craic, and frozen snow on the surface of the ice gives us good grip while the ice deep below the two of us makes funny groaning noises.

'Are you all right there, sonny?' my father enquires, shouting his rhetorical question over his shoulder. 'And not a word about this to anyone when you get home, do you hear me now?' I am sworn to secrecy for all time – a difficult restriction to place on a child cycling down the middle of the Grand Canal that winter.

* * *

Downings House is a 9,000 square foot Georgian pile. It is where I was born and where I still happily rattle around. My father bought it and the accompanying one hundred acres of land in 1927 from a Captain O'Keeffe who in turn had acquired it as a gift from the Free State for his gallant efforts fighting in the Civil War and putting down the republicans. Truth to tell the good captain was not supposed to sell the property at all as one of the conditions of his acquiring it in the first place was that he held on to it for his lifetime. But of course, Ireland being Ireland, rules are only made for breaking and in any case the captain wanted to get back to his native Cork. So my father bought the house and land from O'Keeffe for the princely sum of £1,250.

At one time this big square block of a place would have been a petty landlord's residence from where he could preside over the tenants of his 1,000 acres of good lands plus large tracts of high bog with their turbury and shooting rights. In 1801 Alice Bonynge, childless widow of the late Robert Bonynge, whose name we have just seen on the plaque on Healy's bridge, married a widower named Charles Bury who had six children by his previous marriage. They moved into a brand new replacement house, its predecessor having been burned to the ground after the Battle of Prosperous in May 1798. And so for all of the nineteenth century and indeed up until about 1920, Downings House was occupied by four generations of Burys. The second last Bury of Downings, Charles, formed a liaison with his housekeeper, Mrs Weld, with whom he had several children. Charles' wife, a Ní Aylmer from Donadea Castle, haunts the house to this day. Although I have to admit to never having met the lady myself I have it on reasonably good if slightly inebriated authority that sightings of her are quite common.

My father moved in alone. Aged just twenty-seven and fresh back from an education in agriculture at Reading University he set about mixed farming with perhaps more enthusiasm than good sense. He may not have been a great farmer but he was a seriously good writer. It was during this period of his life that he wrote his first great book, *Green Fields* – a pastoral journal about a year's cycle of life on his farm with wonderful tactile descriptive passages about its people and animals, its trials and tribulations. *Green Fields* is a classic and a time capsule always there to remind us of how things once were in rural Ireland in the first half of the twentieth century.

Besides being a seriously good writer, my father played the piano badly and had a good strong singing voice, something that I seem to have inherited from him and that has stood me in such good stead ever since. He was an enthusiastic naturalist and one of my many abiding memories is of him sitting here at this very desk peering down a microscope at some hapless creepy-crawly captured under a slide cover. When he wasn't doing that he was drawing and painting – something he was also quite good at when he put his mind to it. He smoked heavily and drank sparingly, his occasional tipple being a half-pint bottle of Guinness brought up from Fallon's pub in Prosperous, each bottle carefully wrapped in sheets of the *Leinster Leader*. Another occasional tipple of his was a raw egg thrown into a glass of sherry. The egg had to be left intact and the whole lot polished off in one gulp. Many years later I was to eat like this when I fell on hard times in London. Drinking raw eggs in milk or sherry, tossed back in one go, requires a special swallowing knack.

Late in life he described his arrival in Prosperous in the following way:

> One could hardly hear oneself speak with the clatter of corncrakes; the evening skies were a mixture of lilac and roses. In the late hours of night one frequently heard the rattle of a horse and dray going from Blackstick to Dag Weld's, the harness flapping on the horse's back, the chains rattling and the boy or man on board singing at the top of his raucous voice.

On another occasion during the bicentenary of Prosperous village in 1980 and not long before he died he had this to say of his neighbours:

> I have come here tonight especially to thank the neighbours, our native people who were here when I came to Prosperous. In many ways I am a blow in. It wasn't until a little later that I discovered the real assets of this place, the neighbours: Morans, Cassidys, Harrises, Devines, Healys, Currys, Nevins, Mullens, Fr Tom Clark, Fitzpatricks, Ennises, Wards, Regans, Dowds, McDonnells, Condrons, Bagnalls, Welds and the three blacksmiths, Raleigh, Underwood and Bryan. The Mulallys, Skullys, Curleys, Bob and Elsie Dunn, Mrs Loo who kept a sweet shop, Martin Mangan who kept a mitching house at the cross of Prosperous. The Dalys, Cribbins, the Booths, Field, Holts, Kennys, Kanes, Reidys, Dempseys, Monaghans, Gannons and Coffeys, all of these people and many, many more not only contributed to my fifty years' happiness in this place but they also enlightened me on the history of Prosperous, on the cotton mills and on that great triumph of the eighteenth century, the Battle of Prosperous.

In truth though my father bought this place not for the big house but for the land and trees that went with it. The house was then, as it remains today, too large to be practical. He treated it indeed with some disdain using the drawing-room to store oats over the winter months – something that quite alarmed my mother, Alice Curtayne, when she brought her civilising influences to bear on the place in 1936, the year they were married. It must have been quite a rift for her all the same, this gentle educated woman from Tralee, this intelligent hagiologist who could speak four languages and who had been working in Rome before she met my father. And now here she was moving into this large old house with only primitive toilet facilities, no heating, no electricity, no phone nor any other means of communicating with the outside world. And then to top it all the entire place is full of horse feed! It must say a lot for their love for each other that my mother was prepared to put up with all of this in order to be with my somewhat eccentric father.

But in love they certainly were. One year, probably soon after they were married, my father had one of his not infrequent brain waves. Picking a moment when my mother was temporarily absent from the place he went out into the field behind the house and dug a shallow trench, which spelled out the name 'Alice'. Into this trench he sprinkled snowdrop bulbs, then covered the whole shebang up and said nothing to anyone. Then the next February around St Bridget's day my mother was led by the hand to an upstairs window. Below in the late winter grass and written in large white letters of flowers was her name. Wouldn't anyone put up with some oats on the floor of the drawing-room with that kind of romantic carry-on in the place? Those flower letters were there until quite recently when someone inadvertently dug them up while creating a vegetable patch.

Over the years bits and pieces were added to the house to make it more liveable-in. For example a proper bath and toilet were installed at an early stage, together with a water heating system by way of a back-boiler away down in the old kitchen in the basement. It sounds primitive to us now of course but at least, even if it was after much huffing and puffing, one could eventually climb into a bath of heated rainwater harvested from the roof. It was a bit discoloured but otherwise it was fine. Other than this, luxuries were in short supply. Heating was by way of log fires that never seemed to go properly. Smelly oil heaters augmented these poor fires. Cooking was done over an anthracite-driven Aga and night lighting, such as it was, came courtesy of hissing Tilly lamps and wobbly candles. I often wondered how we managed to avoid burning the place down because on many an occasion it was a near miss.

If you never lived through these times of relative hardship then you could never realise just what a miracle rural electrification was when it eventually did come around in the early 1950s. One day you had a hissing dangerous 25-watt Tilly lamp that took ten minutes to get going. The next day there was a switch on the wall inside the door and a naked 100-watt bulb hanging from the ceiling; the mere act of just switching this thing on and off was pleasurable in itself. One day Margaret Hannon was down in the basement slaving over a washboard and a red bar of Lifebuoy soap the next day she was loading a washing machine, albeit a basic one.

Everyone in those days was an 'electrician'. All you had to do was call yourself an electrician and that's what you were. Everyone all at once and together wanted to have their house wired for the 'electric' and there simply were not enough properly qualified men around to keep up with the demands. The two fellows that 'wired' our house brought the power into the house via a hole bored through the window frame and then carried it along on top of a picture rail to drop down each side of the fireplace, one a socket, one a light, both wired back to a single fuse. In those primeval days of rural electrification nobody bothered about casing the wires and as for conduits or chasing the wall properly – you must be joking. 'Forget about it, we're too busy can't you see.' Whatever inspection there was before you got connected up in those early days of rural electrification must have been of the most perfunctory. 'Ah sure it will do grand so it will' kind of stuff. It's a wonder we weren't all electrocuted in our beds.

The next great boon to come around to us 'living down the country' was of course the telephone. It mattered not in the least that it was a big contraption of a yoke bolted to the wall with a windy up handle on it. Nor did it matter one whit that in order to work the thing at all you first had to call up Rita Hughes over in Robertstown who would, provided of course that she was in the mood to and that you had not interrupted her supper or her praying, get the number for you and put you through. It mattered little also that the same Rita had carte blanche to listen into any conversation that you might care to have, however private or intimate. Nor did it seem all that important that she could let it slip to someone else what she had heard you say to your least favourite auntie (although she swore on a stack of bibles that she would never actually do this). None of these things mattered at all. All that truly mattered was that we were now at long last able to reach the outside world and that our city cousins would now have to stop laughing at us and callings us Culchies with no phones. Electricity running along the picture rail and a primitive phone system brought us into the twentieth century, fifty years behind everyone else. But what matter. We had indeed arrived.

We never had a radio either in those early years as a young family. This seems extraordinary now. My father was a frequent broadcaster on programmes like *Down the Country* with Fred Desmond (Des Fricker) but when he wanted to hear a recording of himself on the radio he had to go down to a neighbouring cottage where two bachelor brothers, Jack and Paddy Graham, lived and never spoke to each other. When they wanted to communicate with each other they used the dog Shep as an intermediary. Jack might say to Shep: 'I'm going off to the match now, Shep, and I will be back in a few hours.' And of course Paddy would hear this and it was as good as if Jack had spoken directly to Paddy – something he had not done for seventeen years and had no intention of doing ever again. Here my father could listen to himself on the wireless on a big Pye receiver driven by a wet and dry battery.

* * *

When I was around three years old, before the devil bit me on the elbow and before my cycle down the Grand Canal, I contracted diphtheria – an infectious disease that at that time would have carried a mortality rate of about twenty per cent. So it was worrying enough for those with the good sense to worry. It is a disease that's now eradicated in this part of the world thanks to vaccinations and it is one that I never encountered myself as a doctor in twenty-five years of general practice. The general practitioner who was called to this house was a small dapper little man from Edenderry – Dr Michael Fay. Although I suspect he had a shrewd idea about what was going on himself, Dr Fay nonetheless brought in a second opinion in the form of county physician Dr Jack Ryan from Naas. I can remember the two of them standing over my bed dressed in their three-piece dark pin-striped suits with watch-chains and waistcoats, poking at me and looking worried. But I was impressed all the same. I often wonder if it was this early childish impression of doctoring that drove me towards that profession as an adult.

As for the diphtheria itself I was carted into the 'fever' section that Naas General Hospital had in those days. I have a clear memory of standing up in a cot and throwing a penny that someone had given me out onto the floor and a nurse coming in and picking it up. So I can't have been too bad and after all antibiotics had by this stage reached some degree of sophistication and diphtheria is, when all is said and done, a simple, if occasionally lethal, bacterial illness. I was never in hospital again as a patient until forty-five years later when in 1990 I was rushed into hospital to have the bullet removed from my right hip joint.

A frequent visitor to this house during my childhood was my only living grandparent, my father's mother who we called 'Gracky'. Gracky was an O'Mara from Limerick and a major shareholder in O'Mara's Bacon, at the time a hugely successful bacon-processing company long since subsumed into some bigger conglomerate. Often as not accompanying Gracky would be her spinster daughter Mary. Out in the kitchen the 'maid', who we may have had to dress up and bring in for the day, entertained their driver to hot scones and jam.

Mary was sophisticated, spoke with a posh accent and smoked Craven A cigarettes through a long slim cigarette holder. Gracky smoked Churchill, a seriously strong cigarette much favoured by truck drivers. And my father Stephen smoked Sweet Afton. So they'd be all puffing away there beside the big log fire in the drawing-room and drinking real coffee brewed over a methylated spirits burner. This strong stuff was drunk out of tiny little blue cups with a sugar lump added. You held these cups with your little finger sticking out. There would be a decanter of sherry also doing the rounds and they'd all be giving out about this and that and wasn't it so hard to get any kind of decent domestic help these days and how do you all stick it down here in the country in this old, cold house. And when they had all finished moaning and whining they'd get back into their chauffer-driven Chrysler and have themselves whisked off back to Milltown Road whence they had come and a collective sigh of relief could be heard escaping through the roof of Downings House.

But to be fair there were return visits by us to them as well. They lived in a big Victorian house on Milltown Road called Green Fields – it's still there. This place smelled of Brasso and polish and mains gas from the Pigeon House. It smelled too of lavender and eau-de-cologne. We would go up for the strawberries and cream – an annual event. Out in the back garden there were many wonders but none greater than the enormous pear tree that always seemed to have big ripe juicy yellow pears scattered out on the ground from its massive boughs.

Other frequent visitors to this house were the St John's as we called them because they lived in a house in Terenure called St John, a place long since razed to the ground. These were six first cousins, five sons and one daughter of my father's older brother Michael who was later to serve as Irish ambassador to Spain. These cousins were wild and funny and used to give our farm animals a hard time – they not being used to them. There was also this attitude, one that drove my father wild, that they being from the big city and we being country bumpkins, they by right as it were had to be the smarter. My uncle Michael was much given to advising my father on matters agricultural – an exercise that went down like the proverbial feed of crubeens in a synagogue.

There were a few famous people that would call too from time to time. Kate O'Brien was a life-long friend of my parents as was the writer Maura Laverty. Pádraic Colum, poet and scholar, came down by bus one day. Fr John Hayes, founder of Muintir na Tíre, was also in the house a few times. Then there was a large assortment of priests, nuns and even a bishop (who later went on to become Cardinal John Wright of Boston) who said mass from the sideboard in the hall.

* * *

My early education started off in Prosperous national school in the autumn of 1947. The school was almost exactly one mile away from our hall door. We walked. My first teacher was Mrs McCarthy who also played the pedal organ in the church next door and led us into the *Tantum Ergo*, all of us off key – including the pedal organ. The Prosperous church choir of the 1940s was a breathless and squeaky affair that did very little to lift the mood of general misery of the times that were in it.

Mrs McCarthy was a kindly and patient Cork woman with a big head of white hair and she taught us young scholars our ABC, how to add and subtract, our first few words of Irish and 'Who made the World?' and 'Who is God?', all very profound stuff really. We were in the long room upstairs. It smelled of damp turf ash, damp turf smoke, chalk dust, a hint of stale urine, dirty clothes and ink. We made our own ink and there was a funny smell from it. Mrs Mc-Carthy wore a big woolly jumper to keep herself warm. Turf was thrown into a lean-to shed out the back, a cartload at a time con-tributed by whoever's turn it was to make such a free contribution. In this way the warmth of our classroom on any given winter's day very much depended on the quality or otherwise of the turf that had been donated at that time. A lot of people around Prosperous in those days were very poor and often the turf was damp, the fire in the potbelly stove only barely kindling and the heat from the stove negligible.

In the back yard of the school also there were what passed for toilets, one for the boys and one for the girls. These were in effect no more than planks with a big round hole cut into them and laid across two supports, all positioned over a ditch. I could go into some more detail here but perhaps I had better spare you lest you are of a delicate constitution or planning a nice lunch.

The national school in Prosperous in the late 1940s was a great place for nicknames. You needed to be a bit of a character to qualify for one and perhaps that is why I never did. Most nicknames had the definite article in front of them and so you would have:

The Tiler Ward
The Spider Dempsey
The Traneen Tracy
The Cowboy Mullins
The King Keenan
The Pullet Ward
The Pike Keegan
The Crow Doran
Plunkett Condron
Plureen (meaning a drop) Tierney

It was only boys who were given nicknames. I do not know why it is but girls seemed to escape the practice untouched.

For the next two years I was taught by Kathleen O'Sullivan, also a kindly and patient Kerry woman, a good teacher and tireless community worker. There was corporal punishment in the school at the time of course but I have to say I don't remember much of it being meted out in my direction, but then I was lucky. Had I stayed on longer than the four years I was there, I would eventually have had to face Mickey Brosnan who taught the fifth and sixth classes and whose brutality is still spoken of in hushed tones to this day.

* * *

Looking back now over fifty-five years it is hard to believe the amount of poverty that was around Prosperous at the time when I was going to school there in the late 1940s. I do not remember any-one actually in bare feet but I do remember some poor lads dressed in rags. And what they brought with them for lunch was also very telling. Some, God love them, brought nothing at all and we would share a little of ours with them. For the most part though school lunch in those days consisted of a few slices of batch loaf with a thin spread of homemade blackberry jam on them, no butter and a bottle of cold tea with a bung of newspaper plugged into the neck in place of a proper cork.

Introibo ad altare Dei. Ad Deum qui laetificat juventutem meam.
Judica me, Deus, et discerne causam meam de gente non sancta:
ab homine iniquo et doloso erue me. Quia tu es, Deus, fortitudo mea:
quare me repulisti, et quare tristis incedo, dum affligit me inimicus.

I am an altar boy dressed in white surplice and black soutane. I can speak Latin and my hair is blond. This is where I had my first taste of alcohol and very nice it was too I must say. Nothing like a good swig of altar wine on a winter's morning to give you a bit of a gee up. Drinking is an occupational hazard among altar boys. There may be other hazards too that I mercifully avoided but I have yet to meet an ex-altar boy who didn't have the odd swig of altar wine from time to time. It was one of the very few perks the job carried.

Little Mrs Dempsey is in the sacristy boiling up two big brown eggs on a good turf fire for himself. Fr Mahon is an unhappy little man. He lives alone and may even be celibate, which could account for his briary disposition. In those days we all believed that priests were in fact celibate. If you looked crooked at him he'd ate the headahya. Everyone, altar boys and congregation alike, is afraid of him. Fully-grown men take flight out the church door one Sunday morning with Fr Mahon in hot pursuit. He had already asked them twice to come up into the pews and by God he was going to fix them good. Men have been standing at the back of the church in

Prosperous for 180 years but Fr Mahon was going to put a stop to such irreverence. He seemed to have absolutely no concept of the natural formation of an audience. Some people are only happy if they are right up in the front, others, perhaps slightly claustrophobic, prefer to stand at the back near the door. That is the natural behaviour of an audience or congregation but Fr Mahon is too insensitive to see it that way.

'Ave, ave, ave Maria. Ave, ave, ave Maria.' Mrs McCarthy and her troop of asthmatics are doing their best to defuse the situation.

Fr Mahon kept Springer dogs and shot pheasants over them. He never invited anyone to go with him which must have meant that half the birds raised could not have been shot at since nobody, not even a celibate priest, can be on both sides of a ditch at the same time. Rough shooting pheasants around Prosperous always requires two people, one to each side of the ditch, shooting on one's own is a waste of time. But of course while the rest of us mortals could only shoot on lands where we had permission, Fr Mahon could shoot where he liked.

A man used to go to Mass there in those days called Luke Curley. Poor Luke suffered from the most awful epileptic seizures. So bad and so frequent were these attacks that men were afraid to be near him at Mass in case he'd have one and they would have to look after him. He died as a result of the same epilepsy in the end. He had been on horseback when a seizure struck him. In those days this condition was treated with phenobarbitone but you could only push that so far before the side effect of doziness would make the treatment worse than the disease. Had he lived a little longer newer treatments would have been available that were much more effective and safe.

In that church in Prosperous at the time the women all wore hats or scarves on their heads and sat or kneeled on the right-hand side of the church as you look up at the altar. All the men bared their heads and stayed over on the left. This convention was non-negotiable and adhered to with a grim rigidity. It mattered not in the least that you may have been lovers, husband and wife, mother and son, father and daughter. Rules are rules and it was women to the right, men to the left and that was that.

Dominus vobiscum. Et cum spiritu tuo. The bells of the Angelus are calling to pray. In sweet tones announcing the Sacred Ave.

CHAPTER 3

Some Schooling

N ow with national school in Prosperous safely behind me I am about to be shipped off to Ring College down in Waterford for a full year's boarding there. The year is 1951 and I am nine years of age and a bit young I think to be wrenched from the security of family life. As with everything else in the Ireland of this time, things have not been going particularly well at home on the farming front. Men have been let go and the money is tight. On the national front things are even worse with thousands of Irish people emigrating to the UK each month. We do not know it then but this is the start of a whole new wave of emigration, the time of the vanishing Irish.

There is a well-known Waterford lilt that translates like this:

I was a day in Waterford
There was wine and punch on the table
There was the full of the house of women there
And myself drinking their health.

Having been in Ring College for one full month everyone was expected to switch to speaking Irish exclusively. Being caught speaking English after October was an offence that was taken very seriously indeed. It used to be an expelling offence in the school's earlier days but the fact of the matter was that when I was there times were hard all over Ireland and the owner of Ring, An Fear Mór, was finding it difficult enough to fill the school. Certainly he could hardly afford to go expelling people found speaking English or he would soon be losing revenue. My memory of it is that the 'speak Irish only' rule was as much honoured in the breach as in the observance. Certainly in the classrooms only Irish was spoken. But outside on the playing pitch or in the handball alleys it was a mixture – Irish out loud and English under your breath.

An Fear Mór was indeed aptly named. He looked a tall gangrenous and rather gaunt figure to me, a nine-year-old looking up at him. In some ways there was a de Valera-like cut to him. But for all his height he was a gentle man and known to be a patient teacher. He devoted his life to the promotion of the Irish language and the founding of his own Irish college.

Whenever I think of Ring College I feel cold and hungry. The food was sparse and inadequate. Breakfast was a small bowl of porridge with skimmed milk and sugar. It had a funny kind of old taste to it that I can't quite describe. This was followed by bread and butter and jam. Only on Sundays did we get a 'fry' consisting of one bit of black pudding, a sausage and a hard-fried egg. During the week we lined up mid-mornings at a window where we were each handed a slice of buttered bread. Many of us would take this back into the classroom and toast it on the potbellied stove using a ruler as a toasting fork. All of us in that class had burned rulers and nobody seemed to have seen fit to outlaw this rather dangerous culinary activity.

Lunches and evening meals were not much better. Burned vegetable soup was a great favourite. I can still smell it. 'Cheffy's Vomit' we used to call it. But as the man was not able to rustle up a bit of soup without making a mess of it you can imagine what his other efforts at high cuisine were like. Meals were presided over by Mícheál O'Donal who sat up at a raised table, a leather strap sticking out of his back pocket. This strap was used on the hands of any young offenders although in truth corporal punishment was not a big feature in the college at that time. Every Wednesday we were released into free Ireland and marched in line up to 'the store' a mile away where we were allowed to spend one shilling each. A slab of Cleeve's toffee was how a lot of us used up our budget because it would last you for most of the day. You had to find a fairly heavy stone to break off a bit from a slab of Cleeve's.

We slept in long dormitories with lockers at the end of the beds. You had to keep your locker very tidy and polish your shoes regularly. The boy in the bed next to me composed a song in Irish to be sung to the same air as 'Carricdone'. The first line went: 'Tá an gruaig ag fás ar mo Mícheál.' 'The hair is growing on my Michael'; an event in his young life that he clearly thought was worth capturing in song. What came after this first line I am not at all sure but I suspect that he may well have run out of inspiration at this point. What a pity. Nor can I say what turn this young bard's life took when he graduated from Ring College. For all I know he may well have become a lyricist of the punk rock industry for clearly he showed great early promise in this particular genre.

Looking back on it now I have to say that my year in Ring was not a particularly happy one. I was too young to be away from home and having to learn everything through Irish had its own unique disadvantages. In fact the whole thing put me back for a full year because when I presented myself to the brothers in Naas having come out of Ring, I was put back into fourth class because I could not do long division. My age would have rightly had me in fifth class. So in effect I had lost a whole year. You might say so what's the big deal? All I can say is that it did affect me. At the end of the day this meant that I was nineteen doing my leaving certificate whereas everyone else was seventeen or eighteen and I never really felt good about that.

I did learn something in Ring College though. I learned the rudiments of tin-whistle playing and an appreciation for Irish singing and these were to be a considerable advantage to me in later life and indeed right up to this day.

* * *

For the most part I cycled the seven miles into the Christian Brother's moat school in Naas and back again each day. And while this may have been tough at the time, I believe it has served me well since in that I have always been blessed with a level of fitness and energy that in truth I do very little to deserve. You would not get a ten-year-old boy today to cycle fourteen miles a day and, even if you could, it would be most unsafe for him to attempt it. But back in 1952 the roads around here were all but empty. You could go all the way from Downings House along the canal to the moat school in Naas and not see four cars during 'rush hour'. Sometimes I could get in behind a tractor pulling a load of turf or hay and you would get kind of sucked along and that was great. If it was raining I had this cape that went over the body and over the handlebars and I wore a water-proof hat on my head and really there was no big deal about any of this. I have no memory of ever being cold on that long bicycle journey.

My first great setback on entering that school was being put back into fourth class as I have already mentioned. After that everything was fine really. The Irish Christian Brother's Schools, founded by Edmund Rice during the first decade of the nineteenth century, had a reputation of being very rough and liberal with their corporal punishment. I say 'had' because Christian Brothers are now practically extinct. Unfortunately all we ever seem to hear about the Christian Brothers these days is when yet another of its elderly community, white-haired, stooped and wearing civilian clothes, is dragged in front of the courts to face yet more charges of a paedophilic nature. This is an absolutely catastrophic end to the teaching order because it tends to completely overshadow the memory of the many good and decent men who joined the brothers over the past 200 years. There have been very few new recruits in Ireland to the brothers in the past five years. They are in effect almost finished, almost extinct.

The brothers had, as I say, a reputation for being somewhat brutal but I saw none of that in Naas during my time there. I had Brother Joyce, Mr McCarthy, known to the boys as Stalky, and Brother Tynan, and I have to say that each of these men in their turn was a good teacher who treated us all with respect.

During my three years in the CBS in Naas my two sisters, Bridget and Catherine, were away in Dominican College, Wicklow while my brother, Davoc, was a few classes ahead of me in CBS Naas and later was away in agricultural college in Gormanstown. So for much of this time I had the place at home more or less to myself, which suited me fine. Both my parents were of course always writing. My mother was working on a book to be titled *Irish Saints for Boys and Girls* while my father was working on his second book titled *All Ireland*.

All Ireland, first published in 1956, was a major undertaking and is a beautifully written and illustrated guidebook to all of Ireland. But that's the problem. If the book has any faults it is that it is too delightfully written to be just a guidebook while not being insipid enough to be a complete guide of all Ireland, if you can follow. My father can't seem to sacrifice any literary art for the merely practical and we end up with a book perhaps better suited to the bedside table than the glove compartment of the car. But does that matter? Dip into his book anywhere and you will see what I mean:

> *Having tried making territory in every shape and form, the weary world brings its experimenting to a conclusion in county Cork. Gougane Barra is a deep tarn held in a cup of crusty mountains: on the open side the infant river Lee frolics out of its rock-ribbed, mountainous nursery.*

* * *

It was around this time too that Davoc and I tried our hands at the hard labour that footing turf really is. During the summer of 1955 Bord na Móna, up the road from us here, was paying very good money on a piecework basis. We were trying to get enough money together to buy a bicycle each. In those days a good new bicycle cost in the region of £14. In Bord na Móna they were getting thirty shillings per plot of turf footed. A plot comprised one acre of machine cut turf lying tightly knit in long rows flat on the ground. So if you managed to foot say only ten plots each you had your bicycle. A good worker could easily foot a plot of turf a day and get well started into a second one. It all sounded fine in theory. Given that we worked like everyone else we should have our bicycles in about two weeks' time.

But with us there was absolutely no chance of success. Footing turf is the most soul destroying, boring and backbreaking work that I have ever put my hands to. There we were, young, fit and motivated and between us we staggered to foot a half a plot a day. If you do not do this properly the ganger Con Burke might come along and kick down your day's work. There are no short cuts, no tricks of the trade. You just get on with it and do it and do it right, as they would have said at the time.

You turn the first two sods upside down on the ground about a foot apart at their centres. The next two sods also get turned ground-side skywards and are placed horizontally across the two on the ground, noughts and crosses fashion. Thus you build the foot up until it is five sods high and therefore contains ten sods of turf in all. Now you move along in a straight line and repeat the performance and then repeat it about 300 more times that day. The dried surface of the turf is hard and abrasive and wears down the skin of your fingers. Only cissies wore gloves in those days. A good footer would only take thirty seconds per foot. It would be much easier and quicker if you did not have to turn each sod as you proceeded but then Con Burke is only about six plots up to your left and is reported to be in a particularly bad humour today. Con was actually a patient of mine twenty-five years later and I got to know him as an absolute gentleman and not at all like the feared ganger he appeared to be to us.

After about a week of this we had to concede defeat. In order to foot turf in the way that some of the people around us were doing it, I think you would want for more than a new bicycle.

* * *

In the autumn of 1956 I started to board in the Dominican College, Newbridge for what was to be a five-year stint. Situated on a bend of the river Liffey and with a decent view of the Dublin and Wicklow mountains in the distance, Newbridge College first opened its doors to students in 1852. My first day there was a cool, bright and breezy autumn day. There was a lot to get used to. Qualifying as a 'local boarder' I was to be allowed go home on all bank holiday weekends and, later, on most Sundays. This took away a lot of the tedium and loneliness of being a boarder, that and the fact that I already had a taste of boarding in Ring College. During those first few days many of my fellows students were homesick and displaced but after a few days most people more or less settled down and accepted their lot.

At that time the college was divided into two separate sections – a junior school for first, second and third-year students and a senior school for fourth, fifth and sixth-year boys. I was to spend two years in junior school and three years in the senior house across the courtyard. This actually was a sensible arrangement because it tended to reduce the bullying and other nasty ancilliary activities not unusual to boarding schools of the day. Each year then in turn was divided up into an A class and a B class for the less academically endowed. Throughout my five years in Newbridge College I never made an A class but it didn't bother me all that much.

There were far more priests than lay teachers there at this time. Many of them carried colourful if not always flattering nicknames. There was the religious teacher, Fr Cassidy, who was called Hopi as in Hop-Along Cassidy. There was Fr Curtin, who we called the Gimlet, because of his piercing eyes. There was a nasty little Corkman who taught mathematics and who was given the nickname Snitch which suited him nicely. There was the French teacher, Fr O'Donovan, who was named Ghostie because, in his white habit and with his gaunt expression, he looked like your quintessential ghost. There was an unfortunate and very elderly little lay teacher called Snotters. Poor old Snotters would stand on the threshold of the classroom with his fingers clasped together in front of him under his chin and he would kind of sway backwards and forwards as if not knowing whether to come in or go out of the room. There was a fellow in my class called Fergal McAuliffe and he could do a great take off of Snotters' way of coming into a classroom.

And then of course there was the Coot, Fr Henry Flanagan, the best teacher that I ever had in my life. If I am ever asked for just one thing to justify my five years spent in Dominican College, Newbridge, paid for by my hard-pressed and far-from-well-off parents, then I would cite the Coot. But then of course he taught my best subjects. He taught and conducted the choir, something I served in every year, first as an alto, later a tenor, not because I was a goody-two-shoes but simply because I enjoyed singing. Then he directed the annual Gilbert & Sullivan opera, something I was also very much involved in every year – *Patience*, *The Mikado*, *The Pirates of Penzance*, *HMS Pinafore* and *The Yeomen of the Guard*. He taught English and art and directed the arts and craft club. In this club, which I joined on my very first day in Newbridge, I learned how to turn wood and the rudiments of cabinet-making, skills that have been useful to me all my life. My friend Fergal McAuliffe made a flat-bottomed boat that we later took down the Liffey as far as Yeomanstown.

One of the nice things about Newbridge was that you were not forced to play rugby – a game for which I had very little talent anyway. So, while my mates may have been practising the scrum or line-outs, I might be turning a large salad bowl in the arts and crafts club. I am not saying that one activity is in any way superior to the other. All I'm saying is that in education, rather than regimentation, latitude in allowing students to find their own niche is very important.

The Coot taught us English in fifth year and asked us to write an essay about a train journey I think it was. I remember then, for the first time in my life, using some descriptive passages and creative ideas and actually enjoying writing. What I produced was no masterpiece of course but Fr Flanagan thought it was good enough and he read it out to the class and congratulated me. I do not believe that all teachers fully understand the importance of a little praise now and again. That year I was given a gold medal for essay writing and my confidence was renewed for all time. It is the small things and rare moments like that that education should be all about, not brilliant marks and six honours in the leaving certificate.

While in Newbridge I also joined the FCA or Forsa Cosanta Áitiúil, Ireland's reserve army. The other fellows in our class used to laugh at us and say that we were in the Free Clothing Association. But they could laugh away. I was in the FCA for three years and enjoyed every moment of it. I fired the Lee Enfield .303 rifle, the Vicker's Submachine Gun and the Bren Gun. Every summer we went to Kilkenny to the army's annual training camp where we were sent on field manoeuvres, learned about combat tactics, field communications, ceremonial drill and how to work the butts under the huge targets to signal to the marksman 500 yards back where on the target their rounds were hitting. After a day of that you would eat a horse. If you misbehaved you were sent on 'fatigues': peeling potatoes for a day or some such demeaning activity. All of this gave me great insight into army life, enough to know that it was not something I would ever want to get into as a career.

In sixth year I was in the debating society and this was something else that stretched the imagination and taught one how to assemble one's argument and present it in a persuasive way. That year too we had a concert at which I sang a song called 'Whistling Phil McHugh', a Percy French song but by no means one of his better ones, wherever I got the idea from:

> Now whistling Phil McHugh has come over from Dunlahy
> And we don't know what to with Miss Mary Ann Mulcahy.

Oh stop please, this is embarrassing. Let's have no more of that. But the point here is that this was the first time that I ever stood up on a stage and sang a song to a real live audience and I must say my audience was most gracious in their applause.

* * *

At home both parents were still beavering away at their typewriters. It was during these years also that my mother made her three lecture tours of the United States. Each tour would last six to eight weeks and take her around most of America, east to west. Her venues were in the main third-level Catholic institutions and her subject was the lives of saints – mostly Irish saints I think. They were fairly punishing schedules and by the time she was finished she would come home absolutely exhausted. But they were also very lucrative and quite frankly money in our house was always pretty tight what with four of us in boarding school more or less all at the same time and writing being the main source of income. Later in life I would learn all about trying to put children through boarding schools myself. It's no joke. In many ways America and my mother may have saved the day.

My mother had a wicked sense of humour. We had a French lad staying with us one of those summers when I was in Newbridge. He was with us as an exchange student to learn English. His name was Jean Pierre and in fact his English was very good except that he was very fond of using the word 'completely' for some strange reason. In a huckster's shop down in Prosperous there was this elderly frail old lady known as Cis Cribbin. In addition to being very old Cis did not make things any easier for herself by having a lighted cigarette dangling from the corner of her mouth from dawn until dusk every day of the week. Her hair, which otherwise should have been white, was now being constantly smoked into a streaky yellow colour. When Jean Pierre first saw this apparition he got a bit of a fright. That evening at supper he was heard to remark: 'Poor Cis Cribbin. She is completely old and yellow.' On hearing this mother took a fit of the giggles from which we thought she would never recover. Indeed, whenever she was reminded of the story later she would chortle to herself for ages. Her take on it was that it must be bad enough to be old but to be completely old and completely yellow at the same time was all just too much.

These years were the heydays of Muintir na Tíre, the rural organisation for community improvement founded by Fr John Hayes from Bansha in county Tipperary. My father was a passionate supporter of this movement and founded a Muintir branch in Prosperous at a very early stage of the organisation's evolution. Today there is a line of maturing lime trees running down the side of the street across from Larry Keogh's public house in Prosperous that still bears testimony to the work of those early Muintir people.

Muintir na Tíre held an annual conference called rural week. These for the most part took place in boarding schools then emptied for the summer holidays. They were innocent enough kind of gatherings, each evening ending with a kind of freelance meeting called a fireside chat. Here people were encouraged to bring up for debate more or less any subject that occurred to them other than religion or politics which were both statutorily barred. Apart from these there were the usual home-grown concerts and céilí dancing after the more serious stuff during the day. There was no alcohol available on site, something that didn't bother me in those days. For a young teenager rural weeks were fertile grounds for opportunities to meet the opposite sex and it was at such a venue in Carlow that I first fell in love, with a girl called Phyllis. After that Phyllis used to write to me in Newbridge College on a regular basis, her letters arriving hidden in the pages of the *Carlow Nationalist*. All letters were screened going in and out of the college. When I wanted to reply to her I had to give my letter to a dayboy or non-boarding pupil who would post it from outside. A lad called Hughie Garret, God bless him, always obliged me in this underground activity. These love-letters from Carlow were very important for sustaining sanity during those otherwise trying times.

Finally then along comes our sixth and final year and I am made one of six prefects who are given minor authoritative roles to play like overseeing the picking up of litter. I share a room with Fergal McAuliffe on the top storey of the new wing. One evening Fergal announces that he thinks he has a vocation to become a Dominican priest. I never then or since actually believed in the concept of 'vocation' so this was all a bit odd. I mean if you think that you are cut out for the weird life of priesthood then that's fine, just get on with it. But what's all this about a calling from God and where is there any evidence to support such a concept?

Under the direction of the Coot we put on a version of *The Pirates of Penzance* and then, six months later, the leaving certificate examination is upon us. In this I failed Latin and French but passed all other subjects easily if without any particular distinction. There was no points system for entrance into third-level education in 1961 so the pressure to get great results in your leaving certificate did not really exist and certainly not to the extent that it does today some forty-plus years later. That said however, the leaving certification examination was a defining moment in the lives of everyone who sat it.

I still have a recurring nightmare about the leaving certificate. In the nightmare typically I have failed in Irish or in maths but this failure is not unearthed until after I have graduated as a doctor. Because of this I have in effect failed the leaving certificate examination and should never have been allowed to enter medical school. Therefore in effect I am not a doctor at all and will need to go back and repeat the whole thing again from start to finish.

I know that this recurring nightmare of mine makes no real logical sense but then is that not the very nature of all or at least most dreams? The point here I think is that there are some defining moments in all of our lives that are of such a magnitude as to switch on a recurring sleep thought that stays with individuals for the entirety of their lives and the leaving certificate examination is such a defining moment. It is nice to wake up from a nightmare like that and know it was only a bad dream.

* * *

Now it is the summer of 1961 and all is well. My long years as a boarder in Newbridge College and the leaving certificate are at last well behind me and this, combined with the sunny, warm weather, induces a certain mild and contained euphoria that I can still feel to this day. My father has not yet developed the rheumatoid arthritis that was soon to blight his health in his declining years. In the back of the *Irish Times* my mother spotted an ad from an elderly gentleman living on the coast road beyond Dalkey. This wealthy old man seeks a young driver to drive him around the continent in return for all expenses paid and a small lump sum. It is a good deal. I have never been outside Ireland before in my short life and this seems a golden opportunity. We agree to meet outside the parade ring at the Curragh race course where the Irish Derby is being run and, after a very brief interview I am hired, just like that. Would that everything in the life to follow were to be so simple.

Within ten days I am walking up the gravelled driveway of a magnificent house overlooking Dublin Bay. This place smells of money. My boss is a frail, thin, old man with a handsome face and thin silver hair. He seems to live alone but that is none of my business. The car is a Zephyr Ford in very good order and we travel down to Dun Laoghaire to take the mail boat across the Irish Sea to Holyhead. There were no drive-on ferries those days. The few cars are loaded on one at a time using a crane and rig. I am free at last. Free of Ireland, free of Ring College, free of the brothers and free of the Dominicans. Free. France, Austria, Germany, Italy, Switzerland and Alpine passes – the Gotthard, the Grimsal and the Furka – all lie ahead. First stop is Paris and the Folies Bergère where I see more naked female flesh than is perhaps good for me. The next day we visit the vineyards of Rheims and the First World War burial grounds of the Somme where my uncle, Richard Curtayne, was killed in action. I cannot find his name and the old man is rushing me.

There are however two not so minor problems. The first is that we are driving a right-hand drive car through countries where we must keep to the right-hand side of the road. I was not a particularly experienced driver at the time so travelling was a bit strained and difficult particularly when it came to passing out other slower road users. The second problem is perhaps more serious.

My boss and travelling companion is not a well man. He suffers from a condition known as tic doloreaux, or trigeminal neuralgia; often, though not always, a painful legacy of shingles or herpes infection. It affects the fifth cranial sensory nerves supplying one or other side of the face. It is more common in women than in men and rare below the age of sixty. Today it is a curable or at least a controllable condition. Then it was not. The pain comes in spasms. This, not unreasonably, made my elderly travelling companion edgy and for most of the time not great company. Talking triggered the painful darts so conversation had to be limited to that which was essential for travel only. I, a mere nineteen-year-old youth, was perhaps not the best at understanding all this and responding appropriately. Maybe the old man should have taken a nice nurse with him to do the driving rather than a gauche young fellow fresh out of school. I'd have brought along a nice nurse were I he.

However, all was by no means lost. Continental foods like deep-fried breaded veal or scampi were all a revelation and a delight to one who had just spent too many years in a boarding school. The scenery at times was breathtaking, most particularly on the Alpine passes. And the wine, served on draught in my bedroom in Cannes was the best I had had since serving mass in Prosperous ten years previously.

CHAPTER 4

Sing for your Supper

Why the Royal College of Surgeons, I am often asked. I have two answers. One is honest and one is not. The dishonest answer is that I had always looked on the Royal College of Surgeons as a proper medical school in that it is the oldest college of its type in Ireland and one of the very oldest medical schools in the world. Moreover, unlike a medical faculty in a university for example, 'Surgeons' only teaches and graduates doctors, dentists, nurses, physiotherapists and pharmacists. Thus it was and indeed remains an institute dedicated to medicine alone.

But while all of that may be true, the real reason why I chose Surgeons on Stephen's Green was that I had nowhere else to go. It may be hard to believe it now, but in order to gain admittance to either the medical schools of Trinity College or University College Dublin in the early 1960s you had to have at least passed Latin and any one language other than English in your leaving certificate. I had failed Latin and passed only English and Irish and therefore, without further study, was not eligible for admittance to any other medical school in Dublin other than the RCSI.

They had fairly easy entrance exams, which I took and passed. Another thing that I had in my favour on application to the Royal College of Surgeons was that I was Irish and we as applicants for places were in a minority. When you looked up at the preregistration lecture theatre of the class of 1961–62, which in those days was just off the back hall onto York Street, the overall skin colour was brown. Then as now people come from all over the world to study at this medical school and in that first year there were only twelve Irish students in that class of over one hundred and twenty pre-med students. These young people came from some twenty-five different countries. And that was to be the first great lesson that I learned at the College of Surgeons in Dublin: that the world is made up of people of many religions, colours, and cultures each totally unique and all equally deserving of each other's mutual respect. If there was any prejudice among us, and I can honestly say that I saw no evidence of any in my seven years in the place, but if there was any, those holding it quickly learned to leave it at home and keep it to themselves.

We in Ireland should be very proud of the cosmopolitan nature of this independent school of medicine. Over the past fifty years Surgeons has seeded thousands of doctors all over this globe bringing relief from suffering to millions of disadvantaged people. Nelson Mandela, on receiving an honorary fellowship of the college a few years ago, put it like this:

> During the dark ages of apartheid your college provided places for many South Africans who were excluded by racist laws from attending medical schools in their own country. Through these doctors you are making an inestimable contribution to the healthcare needs of our people.

A lot has changed in the layout of the College of Surgeons since my time there and a lot has remained unchanged. Unchanged of course is the great Georgian facade that looks out onto St Stephen's Green and that still retains the pock marks of .303 rifle fire it had to endure in the immediate aftermath of the Easter uprising of 1916. Forces of the crown were attempting to evict Constance Markievicz from the building. One has to suspect that they were not great marksmen by the way the bullet marks are splattered all over the place. This landmark building was then, as it remains today, largely given over to administrative and ceremonial function. The upstairs of this building contains many impressive rooms but few more so than the oak-panelled banquet hall where eventually I was to receive my graduation documents. This was to be one of the happiest days of my life.

When I first went to Surgeons, York Street was still full of crumbling and deeply depressing tenement buildings with dark and dank interiors and women leaning out of open windows shouting to each other from across the street. Children ran ragged, poor and too numerous on the street outside. The birth control pill was still a few years away and what I was looking at in fact were the final years of the Dublin of Sean O'Casey and Brendan Behan, the Strumpet City of James Plunkett. We entered the college from York Street aware of the poverty around us. Then, as now, use of the grand front door up the few steps off Stephen's Green was frowned upon. But if for example it were raining we would occasionally chance it and run the gauntlet with the hall porter Mr Cooper who was a big man and an ex-prize-fighter. You didn't mess with Mr Cooper.

On the first day of my pre-registration year, September 1961, I was assigned to seat number 118. Right behind me sat a gentleman who in less than two years' time was to become one of Ireland's most notorious killers and a household name. In fact during those first few months in Surgeons I got to know Shan Mohangi quite well. Early in 1963 Shan was tried and convicted for the murder of his then sixteen-year-old girlfriend Hazel Mullen. But of course it was even worse that that. Panicked at the lethal consequences of his attack on her and finding himself with a body on his hands Mohangi tried to dispose of the body by cutting it up into little pieces and burning it in the basement of his apartment flat under the Green Tureen restaurant in Harcourt Street. It was this gruesome aspect of the tragedy that gave the story and Mohangi such notoriety. Murders were rare enough in the Ireland of the time, cutting up bodies to dispose of them was unheard of.

A story is told of the time that a certain gentleman visiting the Green Tureen was making his way downstairs. As he did so he suddenly encountered a coloured gentleman making his way up the stairs against him. The visitor stepped aside to let the coloured man pass, as he seemed to be in a hurry. The visitor could not help but notice that the other was carrying what looked suspiciously like a human head. Such was the fright that the visitor got that he ran out of the building and all the way around to Kevin Street garda station passing Harcourt Street garda station on the way.

The jury returned a verdict of murder at a time when capital punishment was still on the statutes in Ireland and things were looking very grim indeed for my erstwhile friend and classmate from South Africa. He appealed on the grounds that the whole thing had been a terrible mistake and we were introduced to a new way of dying called 'vagal inhibition'. In evidence, the then state pathologist, Maurice Hickey, said that it was possible to inadvertently kill someone by squeezing him or her, even lightly, about his or her throat. In doing this one may stimulate the vagus nerve and this in turn can cause the heart to stop because the vagus nerve is intimately related to the heart, its sensitivity and rhythm. And thus was born vagal inhibition and Shan's murder conviction was commuted to that of manslaughter and he was given seven years. He served four of those years here in Ireland and was extradited to South Africa to serve the remainder.

This sad tale has a redeeming end. In time Hazel Mullen's mother and her brother both forgave Shan Mohangi and believed that he did not intend to kill poor Hazel. And in time too Shan became a successful South African politician where he now sits in parliament. And we back home were very careful how we kissed and cuddled in the back of the Grafton cinema. If vagal inhibition was all it was cracked up to be then one could never be too careful.

That aside, my first year in Surgeons was something of an unmitigated disaster. Along with many of my fellow Irish I found myself in a class of a-level graduates who had already studied and passed exams in advanced physics and chemistry and biology so all the stuff now going on around us was old hat to eighty-five per cent of this class. Consequently the two sisters, Professor Ethna Gaffney and Eibhlin Kenny, lecturing to us flew along at a cracking rate making it very difficult for the uninitiated to keep up or to take proper notes. The consequence of all this was that I failed physics and chemistry in the June exams that year and failed chemistry again in the autumn exams of the same year. Therefore I could not advance and had to repeat the whole year all because of chemistry. What a bummer.

During that repeat year of 1962–63 I washed test tubes in the biochemistry laboratory of the Richmond Hospital, flew around the place wearing a white coat distributing lab results for all the wards, saw people in pain and others dying and got to know many of the nurses and other staff, with the smell of ether and glycerine and isopropyl alcohol ever in the air. These are the so-called 'hospital smells' and I love them all. This place is a courthouse now but then it was a venerable institution and the headquarters of Irish neurosurgery and thoracic surgery. It was here in 1847 that the first Irish surgical operation was carried out under general anaesthesia. Between operations the surgeons would go across the corridor to their lounge and smoke cigarettes or pipes and drink coffee. While so engaged they kept their gloves and gowns on to save themselves the bother of having to over-vigorously scrub up for the next case. These surgeons were gods to my eyes. I badly wanted to be one of them some day. Among them was Professor Colman Byrnes, a pioneer in thoracic surgery who, within a few months, was to succumb to lung cancer himself. A heavy smoker he died of the disease he spent his lifetime trying to cure.

Also during this fallow year I did little or no study because only chemistry stood in the way of my going on to medical school proper and I intended taking grinds in that for the two months leading up to the exam. Around this time I began to take a serious interest in Irish traditional music and singing. Good songs were very difficult to come by just at this stage. Nobody wanted to know about Percy French or Delia Murphy or Mary O'Hara or the tinker lady Margaret Barry, great and all as these people may have been in their day. The Clancy Brothers and Tommy Makem were on a roll in the US after their debut appearance on the *Ed Sullivan Show* in 1961 but they remained practically unheard of back in Ireland for a year or two yet. They were about the only source of new folk material on record although the records were very hard to come by. My physics notebook contained some of their songs hurriedly jotted down:

When I'm dead and laid out on the counter,
A voice you will hear from below.
Saying send down a hog's head of whiskey
And we'll drink to old Rosen de Beau.

Yes, a major folk-music revolution may be about to explode but it is
important to acknowledge also that many factors, not least of course
the musicians themselves, ensured that in fact interest in Irish folk
music and singing never died out nor for that matter showed any
signs of dying out. The first All-Ireland Fleadh Cheoil was held in
Mullingar in 1951 organised by Comhaltas Ceoltóirí Éireann with
an attendance of some 1,500 devotees. Ten years later the attendance at the same venue was close to 100,000. Prior to the Fleadhs
there were Feis Cheoils – timid little affairs held out in a field with
little girls hopping up and down on the back of a lorry. But at least
they were doing it.

Then there was Gael Linn and all the trojan work that they did
during the 1950s collecting and recording Irish music and songs for
posterity. On this point too one has to mention Ciarán Mac Mathúna and his long series of radio programmes called A *Job of Jour-
neywork*. From the early 1950s right through to the mid-1970s Ciarán
travelled the length and breadth of Ireland collecting and broad-
casting musicians and singers of all levels of talent. He even made
trips to the UK and the USA to chase down and record our musi-
cally talented lost diaspora.

Dominic Behan also was exceptional in singing and composing
Irish folk songs before anyone else and he had a four-track record
out at this time with 'Liverpool Lou' and 'The Patriot Game' among
others on it. And of course the great Joe Heaney from Carna in
Connemara recorded in London in 1960. Joe was way before his
time with a record of his unaccompanied singing of four songs:
'John Mitchell', 'The Rocks of Bawn', 'Morrissey and the Russian
Sailor' and 'The Bold Tenant Farmer'.

Seán Ó Riada's music score for the film *Mise Éire* in 1959 was
also undoubtedly a massive watershed in the revival of interest in

traditional Irish music. This music, used to accompany a film commemorating the Easter Rising of 1916, featured two powerful and classic Irish airs – 'Roisín Dubh' and 'Sliabh na mBan'. These were played on a French horn with Radio Éireann's Symphony Orchestra in full support. The effect was stark and moving, simple yet powerfully effective, making the film utterly unforgettable and bringing it and its music international acclaim.

A few years later Seán Ó Riada was to revolutionise the way group Irish traditional dance music was to be played. With his founding of the group Ceoltóirí Chualann, old style céilí music was given a brand new lease of life. Rather than all the musicians playing together and in unison, as they had to do to get volume for dancing in the days before amplification, Ó Riada broke them up into their integral parts. In this way maybe two fiddles would play the first turn of a reel only to be suddenly joined by all, including percussion, for the second and third turns of that reel. Some people of course didn't like this innovation but then some people hate all changes and want things to stay the same for all time. I loved it I have to say and faithfully followed Ceoltóirí Chualann through a series of five recorded concerts that they held in Francis Xavier Hall off Dorset Street for a radio series later to be broadcast under the title of *Fleadh Cheoil an Radio*. This programme also featured sean-nós singers but few sweeter than the Waterford man, Niclas Tobin.

At this time too the Belfast family, The McPeakes, had played in Dublin and had an LP out. I drew much inspiration from this talented family with their unique sound of concert harp, uilleann pipes, banjo, and guitar and close vocal harmony. Francis McPeake senior, then in his eightieth year, was the only man that I ever knew who sang and played the pipes at the same time. They wrote many classics but few gained more international appeal than 'Will You Go Lassie Go' which they sang in close harmony and with great passion.

Over in America the likes of The Weavers, Pete Seeger and Woody Guthrie were all well-established artists in the American folk idiom with several records to their names. Joan Baez and Bob Dylan were to be the new kids on the block. England too was years ahead of us with the likes of Ewan McColl and Peg Seegers and their London Singing Club and younger singers like Martin Carthy, Maddy Prior and June Tabor. All of this was terrific stuff but not quite what I was really looking for which was older traditional songs, street ballads, sea shanties, sporting songs of English or Irish origin and above all sean-nós or traditional Irish unaccompanied singing in an individual and ornate fashion. All of this was to come cascading down on us within a year or so. This was the lull before the storm.

But if the so-called 'folk revival' in Ireland seemed slow this was due to the fact that interest in, and the playing and singing of, traditional Irish music had never actually waned. It is just that after the so-called revival it all became so much more immediately accessible. But that's all.

But if we were temporally short of records then of course there was always sheet music and songbooks. Of the latter there was one bible called Colm O'Lochlainn's *Irish Street Ballads*. And while this book had been first published way back in 1939, twenty-five years later it was still as vibrant and alive as ever. In addition to the words and music of so many worthwhile folk songs it also had wonderfully amusing wood-cuttings worked through it. Perhaps the best early song to come out of O'Lochlainn's was 'The Rocky Road to Dublin' and first sung by Johnny Moynihan down in the Coffee Kitchen in Molesworth Street:

> *'Twas in the merry month of June when first from home I started*
> *Left the girls in Tuam they sad and broken hearted*
> *Saluted my father dear, kissed my darling mother*
> *Drank a pint of beer my grief and tears to smother.*
> *And it's off to reap the corn, leave where I was born*
> *Cut a stout blackthorn to banish ghost and goblin*
> *With a brand new pair of brogues I rattled over the bog*
> *And frightened all the dogs on the rocky road to Dublin.*

It was great stuff and sung to slip-jig timing. You'd need to be in the whole of your health to face into 'The Rocky Road' but we were and we did and that was the song that was to get me into the Abbey Tavern out in Howth a few months later. I sang and played there for the best part of two years.

* * *

Now it's the autumn of 1963 and John F. Kennedy has come to Ireland and gone home again making us all feel better and proud of ourselves. Nelson's Pillar is still standing but its days are numbered. Thanks to some brilliant grinds that I received from a man somewhere around Kenilworth Square, I understand enough about chemistry to eventually pass all my pre-registration exams. Test tube washing days are over and I was never to fail another exam in this place. Once I got over the Beecher's Brook that was pre-med I never looked back. I am now a real medical student at long last. I am wearing a white coat and I even have a scalpel and I'm dissecting real corpses or cadavers, as we liked to call them.

We proudly walk up and down the length of Grafton Street with *Gray's Anatomy* under our oxters. In the dissecting-room five bodies, three male and two female, are lifted out of their holding tanks of formaldehyde by Christy every morning and laid out on dissecting trolleys. The class is divided up into groups of ten students per body. We are to be in here for a few hours every day for the next two years. Nobody ever explained to us why we are required to cut up dead bodies or if we found such an activity distasteful and repulsive. I believed then as I believe today that medical school anatomy departments are designed to give employment to professors of anatomy who are often failed surgeons themselves. If they serve any other purpose then precisely what that purpose is escapes me.

Of course all doctors need to know some human anatomy. We need to know the names of and the course taken by all the major blood vessels, nerves, muscles and tendons and we need to know their relationship to one another. We need to know about the musculo-skeletal system and how it works. And finally we need to know about the major abdominal and thoracic organs and their relationship with each other. But all of this can be learned from three-dimensional models, MRI scans and illustrations. There is in fact no need to dissect human bodies to learn this stuff. The practice is a hangover from the dark ages of the body snatchers like Burke and Hare. Anatomy was taught to medical students when they had nothing else to teach them. But we foraged on.

The large dissecting-room smells of formaldehyde, decayed human flesh and cigarette smoke. One of my classmates, Anne Dawson, douses herself in perfume every morning before facing into this disgusting place. The women tend to stick together picking away at one body and are largely ignored by the fellows. The women do not smoke or use foul language, the men, by and large, do both. There is absolutely no romance in this place. Any coy notions that any of us may have harboured about the sacrosanct nature of the intimate details to do with genitalia, male or female, can forget about that now for all time. In this room all secrets are exposed and uncovered. This is a place utterly devoid of any semblance of modesty. It must by its very nature be so.

You dissect a body in a planned and organised fashion, section by section. We started in an area in the front inner aspect of the thigh called the femoral triangle. This is bounded on its outer or lateral aspect by the sartorius muscle so called because it is the muscle used by a tailor to bring his ankle onto his opposite knee while cutting cloth. At the apex of the femoral triangle you dissect down to find where the femoral artery, the femoral vein, the great saphenous vein and the femoral nerve all merge together at one point. The importance of this is that it is the exact spot on the front of his thigh where a boner will stab himself with his boning knife should it slip in its downwards course. Such an injury is potentially lethal and needs urgent surgical intervention.

Our *modus operandi* is that one person actually does the dissecting using scalpel and forceps while another reads from *Gray's Anatomy* a description of what is being uncovered. Occasionally our demonstrator Mr Rooney will come along and, using a long curved surgical scissors called a Mayo Scissors, point out this and that. Mr Rooney is a fine teacher but a sad, slight and unhappy figure. I do not think that he enjoys his work. Before he took up anatomy demonstrating he was Kildare county surgeon and rumour has it that he lost his nerve for surgery. Demonstrating anatomy is a long, long way from actually performing life-saving surgery. It is hardly any wonder then that the poor man looks grim and grey.

Grim and grey too is the book from which we read. *Gray's Anatomy* is not exactly a belly full of laughs. There is a photograph of the great author himself on the flyleaf and he looks like an undertaker's assistant. He describes the scrotum thus:

> *The scrotum is a cutaneous pouch containing the testes and the lower parts of the spermatic cords and placed below the pubic symphysis. The left portion hangs lower than the right in correspondence with the greater length of the left spermatic cord. The skin is very thin, of brownish colour and generally thrown into folds or rugae. It is beset with thinly scattered crisp hairs, the roots of which are visible through the skin.*

I do not know whose scrotum Gray is endeavouring to describe here. But as someone who has now had a fairly intimate relationship with some 25,000 of them, I can say he is not describing the typical one. So much for authoritative textbooks.

* * *

Things on the outside world are going very well indeed. The folk revival is now in full swing and there is no end of places to go to. O'Donoghue's pub on Merrion Row is not yet a venue for music and the student architects frequenting it at this time are barred from singing. No singing was allowed in any pub in Dublin in the very early 1960s with the exception of the so-called 'singing lounges' where the Perry Comos and Johnny Cashes chanced their arms in front of a microphone after ten pints of porter. I remember going to such a place in Camden Street once in desperation but they had nothing whatsoever to do with traditional music or singing.

There were perhaps only a few exceptions to this universal ban on live music and singing in Dublin pubs of the day. The Brazen Head Inn on Bridge Street, Ireland's oldest pub and Robert Emmett's watering hole, did allow us to sing and play there. Tony Murray, just released from the Curragh prison camp for his IRA activities, sang 'Henry Joy McCracken' – a song that reminds us, if we need reminding, of the fact that not all Ulster Presbyterians were unionists and that some in fact fought and died for the cause of the United Irishmen and a new republic in 1798:

> An Ulsterman I am proud to be from the Antrim Glens I come
> And although I laboured by the sea I followed flag and drum.
> I have heard the martial tramp of men
> I have seen them fight and die
> Ah lads I well remember when
> I followed Henry Joy.

Mick Dwan from Ennis sang 'The Cliffs of Duneen' and later tried to teach me how to play 'The Kilfenora Jig' on a tin-whistle.

> You may travel far far from your own native home
> Far away ore the mountains far away ore the foam
> But of all the fine places that I've ever seen
> There are none to compare with the Cliffs of Duneen.

There is in fact no such place as Duneen but that hardly matters. The words of the song would place the singer somewhere around Tarbert in north county Kerry where my uncle, Fr Tom Curtayne, is buried beside the church. 'The Cliffs of Duneen' has always held a high place in my repertoire of songs. I love every word and note of it and I later passed it on to Christy Moore who altered the air slightly.

Since by and large we were not allowed to play or sing in pubs, we tended to congregate in places where drink was not sold but where we could give expression to our talents such as they were. The Coffee Kitchen in Molesworth Street, down in a basement, was one such venue. It was here that I met Ronnie Drew for the first time and was immediately smitten by his quite extraordinary talent and great store of unusual songs like 'The Twangman' and 'The Kerry Recruit':

About four years ago I was digging the land
With me brogues on me feet and me spade in my hand
And says I to myself it's a pity to see
Such a fine strapping lad digging turf round Tralee.

Every time I sing that song I think of Ronnie Drew, always immaculately dressed in a dark blue suit and string tie and drainpipe trousers. Such neat attire was a long way from the more usual dress code for folk singers of the day, but Ronnie didn't care. He was always his own man.

In this basement on Dublin's Molesworth Street after the pubs had closed on a typical night you might find Dolly McMahon, Johnny McEvoy, Johnny Moynihan, Andy Irvine, Peggy Jordan scouting for talent, Maeve Mulvany, Trevor Crozier the Trinity student with a stiff leg, Joey Walsh the bodhrán player, Frank Harte the great exponent of the Dublin Street Ballad, Dick Cameron the tall American singer, Al O'Donnell the best singer and banjo player in Dublin until Luke Kelly came along a few years later, Anne Byrne and Jesse Owens, Tom Munnelly later to become state folklorist, Liam Weldon, Ciarán Burke later to join The Dubliners, Amanda Douglas and a whole assortment of musicians and hangers on. Nobody was being paid. Everybody there was giving of their time and talents for no reason other than their love for music and song.

Then there was the Pipers Club in Thomas Street where Rí na Píobairí, Leo Rowsome, was in charge. Leo was a fine musician, an uilleann pipe maker and teacher of that most difficult of instruments. No drinking was allowed in the Pipers Club so it too was a kind of after-hours place. In the three small downstairs rooms great respect was paid to the musicians. Singing was never a big feature in this rather serious folk venue.

The Fiddlers Club across the Liffey on Church Street was another serious Mecca for good music and song. This is where I met Barney McKenna, the banjo player, for the first time. At that time Barney was the only person in Dublin who played Irish music on a tenor banjo and this made him absolutely unique and extraordinarily popular. Barney, apart from his considerable musical talent, was also an extremely amusing man. You would never know what he was going to come out with next. For example during those early days of the so-called folk revival spoon players were in over supply. I remember being at a session with Barney once and he was playing a solo of his called 'The Mason's Apron'. In the background there were at least four spoon players going clackity-clack, some of them out of time. A spoon player or bodhrán player who keeps time is one thing but to have a few of them out of time is hard to bear.

When Barney was finished his piece he turned to me and said: 'Would somebody give those fuckers a bowl of soup?' – equating bad spoon players to prisoners rattling their tin plates on the cell bars looking for food. Another description of a person who tries to play the bodhrán was given to me many years later by Gerry O'Mahony, the box player from Allenwood. He said that a person who was not particularly good on this instrument sounded like a billy goat trying to get out of a wooden barrel. But I think as you might by now have guessed, among Irish traditional musicians the percussion section is often held in some disdain – sometimes unfairly.

Sonny Brogan, the icon of box players, also played at the Fiddlers as did Ted Furey, his son the piper Finbar Furey, John Kelly and Joe Ryan – fiddle players. Maeve Mulvany with her guitar looked after the singing department. Maeve was a very attractive young woman with jet-black hair and she played reasonably good guitar. She liked rebel songs like 'James Connolly':

A great crowd has gathered outside of Kilmainham
With their heads all uncovered they knelt on the ground.

For inside that grim prison lay a brave Irish soldier
His life for his country about to lay down.

Songs like this of course always appeal to a broad base of Irish audiences because of their emotional patriotic content. In that sense then it never really mattered if they were sung well or badly because their content carried them along anyway. I am not saying that Maeve didn't sing them well; it's just that I have always thought rebel songs were a bit suspect.

I never sang or played in the Fiddlers Club. I felt they were too good for me. In any case I was never asked. It seemed to me that the place was alive with Clare migrants.

Peggy Jordan, once described in the newspapers as 'Mrs ten per cent' set herself up as a kind of folk impresario. If you got on her books she would get you gigs in exchange for ten per cent of your takings. That was all very well and grand of course except that in the tiny village that Dublin then was Peggy was a bit surplus to needs and most people looked after their own bookings and held on to their ten per cent. That said though she was a most exuberant, generous and gregarious woman who liked nothing better than to fill her house out in Kenilworth Square with all us singers and musicians. These were the days of the brown paper bag and a dozen bottles of Guinness and all night sessions of music and singing.

It was at one such party in late 1963 that I first met Luke Kelly, then just returned from England. To hear Luke sing in those early days was simply unforgettable. Because I think he may have overreached himself during later concert tours with The Dubliners, his voice, while always good, did deteriorate somewhat in his later life. It was the way in which he attacked a song that really made the hairs stand straight up on the back of your neck. You knew the big note was coming up and you knew that when it did, then by Jasus Kelly was going to go for it. Head held backwards, big head of wild red hair and red goatee beard; once you saw him and heard him you were never ever to forget him. He was an inspiration to us all. His was a voice to aspire to but never equal.

At this time Peggy Jordan was trying to put a group together to entertain the American tourists out in the Abbey Tavern in Howth. Just before this they had a jazz quartet do the job and Ronnie Drew and friends followed this when all the folk singing and music got so popular overnight. A formidable lady, Minnie Scott-Lennon, then owned the Abbey Tavern. Minnie was a slim white-haired woman in her mid-sixties. You'd know by the look of her that she had been something of a socialite in her heyday. She had one golden rule and that was that there were to be no rebel songs in her emporium. Just one rebel song and you were out on your ear. I never asked Ronnie why he left the Abbey Tavern but I do know you had to watch your Ps and Qs where Minnie was concerned. She would be easy to fall out with and Ronnie Drew was never a man to be overly concerned with Ps or Qs for that matter. Anyway I am eternally grateful to him that he did walk otherwise we would never have been offered the job there.

Peggy held the auditions in the Abbey Tavern on a Sunday after-noon and anyone who was interested was asked to go out and strut their stuff. When my turn came along I sang 'The Rocky Road to Dublin', a song that very few were attempting at the time because of the demands it made on your respiratory system. This done Peggy threw her arms up in the air and said 'You're in!!' in that expansive way of hers. This I have to tell you was seriously good news because, provided we didn't rub Minnie up the wrong way, this should be good steady work that would last for God knows how long.

The original team eventually picked to play the Abbey Tavern were:

- Myself, a first year medical student, a singer with lots of volume but not great tone and a mediocre tin-whistle player.
- Dolly McMahon, wife of Ciarán Mac Mathúna and a traditional singer who, when on form had a lovely voice and singing style but was often very nervous about using them.
- Jesse Owens, a male model, guitar player, good singer and all-round smoothy doody.

- Anne Byrne, a singer again with a lovely voice and good repertoire of songs.
- Joe O'Leary, a fiddle player from Ardrahan in south Galway who would recite a long poem about the races at Punchestown that always brought the house down.
- Bob Lynch, a guitar player and singer (mainly in a Calypso style). 'He's football crazy, he's football mad' was one of his offerings. Poor Bob died very young in life.

This group changed a bit over time. Jesse and Anne dropped out early, probably to go on to grasses greener. Peggy Jordan had her inevitable fall out with Minnie Scott-Lennon before we even got started. This meant we would be all ten per cent better off. Joe O'Leary left to be replaced by John Sheehan, future fiddle-player with The Dubliners. Pay was by a strictly equal divide of the door takings on any given night. We often had a full house. The best night we ever had I got eight pounds. Eight pounds in 1963 was very decent money for a short night's work. It was a week's rent for a very upmarket apartment.

Because of the Abbey Tavern I was able to pay for my own accommodation and some of my tuition fees at Surgeons and thus take some of the load off my poor long-suffering parents. I bought a second-hand Heinkel Scooter 175cc, a classic machine that you can still see being driven around Dublin today. To go with this I had a leather jacket made up for me in a leather factory in Rathmines and I wore knee-length leather boots to college where the only dress code was that you had to wear a tie at all times.

Two years of human anatomy and physiology and it's the summer of 1965. At this stage I sit and pass the 'halves exam' and another milestone in my medical education is reached. Gerry O'Sullivan, the dental student from Tralee, and myself pack our bags and head for the big smoke. We are off to London to make some serious money.

CHAPTER 5

The Wild Rover

When the Kerryman was setting off for London he asked his father for some advice that might help him succeed in that difficult place. Having thought about it for a while the father advised his son to look as stupid as he could and call everybody sir. Gerry O'Sullivan, my travelling companion and mentor on this my first working trip to England had a slight variation on this approach to success. Gerry thought it of paramount importance that we not divulge to anyone, either through speech, dress or general demeanour, that we were students. It was his view, and he was very strong on the subject, that if the hiring boss thought for one second that we were medical or dental students then we would get no work. Therefore rule number one: I was to keep my mouth shut, stay quiet and look as stupid as I could and let Gerry do all the talking. Gerry was gifted with a good strong Kerry accent while mine, at least as far as Gerry was concerned, was a bit suspect.

Rule number two, and this was more difficult, we were to look scruffy and have dirty boots and generally try to look like the serious navvies that we were not. The first building site we called to looking for work the man asked me a few questions which I felt obliged to answer, thus breaking rule number one. Then, to make matters worse, my dress code as an unskilled labourer left much to be desired. We got no work that day and it was all my fault.

The next day wasn't much better and things were looking very serious because we were on a limited budget and our money was running out in this hostile place. At this stage we decided to split up on the basis that a single navvy had a better chance of getting work than a brace of navvies, particularly if one of them had a slightly iffy accent and polished shoes. The next day we both found jobs. Mine was out at Heathrow airport where they had just started to build terminal three. I was given a ladder, a lump hammer and cold-chisel. My job was a simple one, one with which I would have thought a half intelligent chimpanzee would have no difficulty. Where poured concrete oozes out between shutterings it leaves a slight ridge on the finished wall surface. My job was to go along and remove these ridges from floor to ceiling, using lump hammer and cold-chisel.

Down below two electricians were working. They had to do some calculations and the one shouts over to the other:

'Hey Mick, what is a third in decimal points?' And Mick says 'Jasus, I don't know.' And I suppose they felt that there was not much point in asking the Paddy up the ladder with the lump hammer and cold-chisel. And, had Gerry been in the vicinity, he would have advised me in no uncertain terms to keep my mouth shut and go on with my work. But I couldn't resist it: 'Point three recurring,' I shout down to them. 'Thanks mate,' they shout back and no more was made of it.

At this stage, although I was working at last, I still had to wait until the end of the week before I'd get my first pay and this was only Tuesday. I had in total about three shillings to survive three days in London. By now I had absolutely no idea where Gerry had disappeared to. He was going to meet some woman or other when last I spoke to him and that was the last I saw of him for the next two months until we were going home. I was abandoned and maybe I deserved to be with my anti-navvy ways. I went out and bought a dozen eggs and a pint of milk and resolved that this would have to do me for the next three days. And so it did. The eggs were knocked back whole with a half glass of milk.

Things gradually improved. I met up with Luke Kelly who was living in London's Finsbury Park at the time with his then new wife Deirdre O'Connell. Luke pointed me in the direction of some possible singing gigs though in fact these did not materialise. I moved from my job at the airport to a better paying one out near Dagenham Docks. Here I worked with a gang repairing and shifting railway lines. This work was extremely hard and consisted of either shovelling ballast between sleepers or lifting old rails onto open carriages. Now of course they would use forklifts. We did it with our bare hands, one man to every three feet of rail, all together now LIFT! We all knew we had to put the effort in because any slacking would only mean more hardship for someone else. We were a team and we worked like a team and, although most of my workmates would have known full well that my credentials as a full-time navvy were a bit dubious, that never caused any problem.

In London that long hot summer, near Shepherd's Bush, I first knew what it was like to be really hungry. Later I enjoyed the delights of a bacon sandwich and a cup of tea before the bus came to take us to the work site every morning. After eight solid weeks of lifting rail and shovelling ballast I do not think that I was ever as fit again in my life. Fit and bronzed and with a few bob in the pocket I am now ready to tackle the second half of my medical education. Summers from here on in would be spent in hospital and I can kiss goodbye to the navvy boots, lump hammer and shovel.

* * *

Third year in medical school is a funny kind of year when you study odd subjects like jurisprudence and medical ethics. This is also the year when we did some psychiatry and pathology. The dental students have now all left us and have gone their separate ways down to the dental hospital in Lincoln Place to drill holes in phantom patients' teeth. Psychiatry takes us out to hospitals and we get to see some real live patients for the first time, albeit incarcerated ones. Even in the mid-1960s psychiatry was still in the dark ages and conducted from grey institutions behind twelve-foot high walls. They no longer chained lunatics to the bedposts but they still kept them under lock and key.

First of all the professor gives us a short address on the two major psychoses, which are manic depressive psychosis and schizo-phrenia. He outlines the major symptoms of each. All of us have mood swings, he explains. We have our good days and bad days, our happy moments and sad moments. That is all very normal and hu-man. But where the manic depressive deviates from the normal is in the intensity of these swings. When patients with this condition are high or manic they think that they can buy out the shops and stay in the most expensive hotels. Nothing is impossible to them. They are expansive and effusive and frenzied and likely to make some desperately wrong decisions. They are also in denial and self-de-structive. When down, they become withdrawn and, in the more extreme form, can become catatonic – a state of total withdrawal from all outside stimuli. At this stage suicide attempts are common and too often successful.

At this point in the proceedings in this lecture hall in Grange-gorman, the professor says that he would now like to introduce us to a classical case of manic depressive psychosis. With that he stands up and taking a big key from his pocket he walks over to a door at the side of the room, unlocks it and admits his poor unfortunate in-dividual. We are then invited to ask this man whatever we like. This is like a scene from *The Elephant Man*. This is my first introduction to a person, or patient if you prefer, in which I am cast in the doc-tor's role and the man is being afforded about as much dignity as one would normally give to a head of cabbage. Why is he under lock and key in the first place? Does he not have some human rights? These were the kind of questions that I would have liked to ask, but wise undergraduates do not make waves.

* * *

We have all left the Abbey Tavern at this stage. We have had enough of it and they have made the venue much larger and the fun has gone out of it a bit. That said, I worked there for the best part of two years for two, three and sometimes four nights a week and never once did I think of this as work. It was always enjoyable and always different. But all things come to an end and besides I was offered a handier number that did not require our having to travel all the way out to Howth every evening. O'Donoghues of Merrion Row, the Mecca itself, were looking for some resident musicians and singers and I am asked if I would be interested. I jumped at the chance.

This place is a phenomenon and an icon and it all happened more or less by chance. It is not as if the owners, Paddy and Maureen O'Donoghue, set out to own an Irish traditional music and singing pub. Far from it. They in fact owned this pub for many years and doggedly persisted with the then Dublin convention of barring all singing in their pub. Singing, for some reason that I never quite understood, was associated, at least in the mind of the publican, with drunkenness and rowdiness and debauchery and no 'respectable' pub therefore ever allowed singing. Indeed neither Paddy nor Maureen had any particular interest in or knowledge of traditional music as they freely admitted themselves. So how did it come about then that they ended up owning the busiest and most famous traditional Irish music pub in the world?

It did not happen by design but rather by stealth. The story goes that one evening towards the end of 1962 Johnny Moynihan was in there and was playing the tin-whistle with his coat over his head so as not to be seen. This serious breach of convention was tolerated for a while but Johnny was eventually asked to cease and desist. But at least the ice had been cracked, if not entirely broken. Now, as we have already seen, a lot of singers and musicians were already congregating in places like the Pipers Club, the Fiddlers Club, the Wren's Nest out in the Strawberry Beds, Johnny Fox's up in the Dublin Mountains and the Coffee Kitchen in Molesworth Street which happened to be only a block away from O'Donoghues. Some of these people were also getting engagements to play in concerts and so on and badly needed a central place to practise. Johnny Moynihan was such a person and he already had a toe into O'Donoghues. Gentle pressure was brought to bear on Paddy and Maureen and a legend was born. Years later Maureen would often say 'God was good to them'. He was indeed but it took some persuading.

Maureen O'Donoghue was a stout lady with a big heart. She administered to her minions from the tiny kitchen that opened into the space behind the bar. Here at lunchtime she presided over an enormous pot of homemade soup and she made up sandwiches to go with this – cheese and tomato, ham or chicken with lots of mustard. From this vantage point she could see everything that was going on, which was usually quite a lot. Maureen never missed a trick. She either loved you or hated you with very little scope in between. You could easily find yourself barred from the pub. For example, wearing your hair too long was a classic barring offence and a rather odd choice given that we all wore our hair longish in those days. It was of course a matter of degree.

But that said I do know for a fact that many is the time that she would discreetly look after people by way of not charging them for soup and sandwiches or indeed the odd pint of Guinness. These might be men who had fallen on hard times or perhaps who may have been the worse for the drink. Alcoholism and ballads are frequent bedfellows.

Paddy O'Donoghue too was a decent kind of a man with old-fashioned good manners and graciousness. He was bald, wore thick black-rimmed glasses and smoked St Bernard's plug tobacco in a twisted pipe. He kept an eye on everything and made sure nobody got out of hand. He worked behind the bar and always had a word for everyone.

We played there three nights a week – Thursday, Friday and Saturday. In our group at the back of the shop there were the Mc-Kenna brothers, Ted and Gordon, who between them played guitar and mandolin. They both also sang, Ted being the better of the two. 'The Blackleg Miner' was one of their favourites:

It is in the evening after dark
That the blackleg miner goes to work
With his corduroys and his dirty shirt
There goes your blackleg miner.

There was Pat Pender, also guitar and vocals, and Pat Stokes who played concertina. There was myself on whistle and singing the odd song and there was Hughie McCormack, the Leitrim fiddle player who spoke fluent Irish. Other musicians like flute player Des Kenny would also join us from time to time. There were no hard and fast rules. Our job was to keep the craic going but if there were enough volunteers from outside our group who wanted to play or sing then that was fine with us too. We just let things roll and the evening often grew organically. We were on free drink for the night plus £3. There was a kind of gentleman's agreement that 'free drink' was a maximum of four pints. There was also a kind of unspoken rule that you did not put it about too much that you were being paid for your contribution. The logic behind this rule was that if people got the notion that certain artists were being paid to sing or play then everyone else would have a right to be aggrieved if they too were not given a free pint having sung 'Fine Girl You Are' off key.

There are a lot of myths that have grown up about O'Donoghues of Merrion Row over the years. One is that The Dubliners played there. One or two of The Dubliners might occasionally, indeed only very occasionally, call by for something or other but they never played there as a paid group. In the early days they may have practised here, not that The Dubliners were ever that pushed about practising. The fact of the matter is that they were too big and this place too small for such a thing to ever happen. It was, as it remains today, a tiny pub with a bar and window space to the front, a small lounge to the rear and that's that. There is no stage, no rostrum, no microphones or sound system. Whatever music there may be at any given time comes from the floor with the singers or musicians depending entirely on the audience's respect as to whether they will be heard or not and, often as not, the audience's respect leaves a lot to be desired. This place is not for the fainthearted.

During the 1960s O'Donoghues of Merrion Row was a 'head place' more so than a traditional musical pub. It was perhaps more interesting to be there around lunchtime on a Tuesday rather than late on a Saturday night when things were mad. At quiet times like these you might get a song from Joe Heaney who might have an audience of four people, all who would have known and respected what he was doing. Joe was an angular and slightly angry Connemara man with that hard Spanish look often found in people from the west of Ireland. He felt very bitter about how he had never really been appreciated in Ireland or by Irish audiences. He had no time at all for Radio Éireann for example and other organs of the state that he thought should have been more helpful. He may well have had a point of course. It is just that he did tend to go on a lot about it. But I loved him. He was such a superb singer, so true to note and ornament singing with his eyes open and fixed to his right in an ancient and sad vernacular that would bring tears to your eyes and make you proud to be Irish. That this man should have ended his days as a porter in a Manhattan hotel is a serious indictment of us all.

Or Seamus Ennis might take out the uilleann pipes just to tune them up before going off onto his next gig and then, while he had them strapped on, he might play a few tunes. It was a workshop, a school, a meeting place, an office, a club and a boozer and eating place all rolled into one. At the street end of the counter was a large message board a bit like the tree outside the New Stanley hotel in Nairobi, where people left messages for each other not knowing if they would ever be received. But the mobile phone was yet to be imagined and landlines and coin boxes were at best problematic, so this notice board was extremely important if, for example, you wanted to ask someone to do a gig on such and such a date. I got plenty of work from this notice board.

There was another thing about O'Donoghue's that was very useful: it was a great place for keeping up with what else was going on in the music world outside of Dublin. Someone in there would always know which was the best Fleadh Cheoil that weekend and who was going to it and you could always go into Merrion Row the Saturday morning of a Fleadh weekend and try to bum a lift. During the 1960s I must have been to at least twenty Fleadh Cheoils in all. Some stand out in my memory above the rest. The All Ireland in Boyle 1967 is a good example. All Irelands were always held over the August bank holiday weekend and those in the know would always stay back until Tuesday when all the cowboys and messers would have gone home. This was the day that the more serious collectors and artists had the place to themselves and my brother Davoc and I were in a pub next door to Grehan's at the top of the square in Boyle. Here by chance we found Willie Clancy and he in full flight. Willie at that time would have been one of Ireland's best known uilleann pipers and it was a great privilege to be in his company and to be at what amounted to a private audience with him.

My brother, who was and still is a better whistle player than I am, played along with Willie as best he could and I played a slow air or two during the afternoon which Willie very graciously acknowledged. The truth of the matter is though that my playing in such elevated company was almost laughable. Willie sang three songs also that afternoon. These were all new songs to me and one was funnier than the next. He sang 'The Gander', 'The Family Ointment' and 'The Taylor Bawn'. To this day I still sing 'The Gander' and would consider it among my top five songs in popularity:

One evening of late as I strayed and I rambled through fields
Where oft times I've wandered with haste and with very quick speed.
I'd be going to a frake where rakes and fractions they do meet
There'd be drinks and strong tae, hot cakes and things that are sweet.

Now this evening was freezing indeed then it was very cold
There was frost in me heels me Boys and there were cramps in me toes
So I thought it no harm to warm me shanks by the fire
Expecting Maura and her daughter that they surely would me admire.

The tae pot came round in spouts we got stuff that was strong
Oh Maura says spake or make a verse of a song,
Old Bill in the corner he cursed and he swore with the fright
Since his gander was stolen and roasted last Saturday night.

Now Bill's gander was old he was noble both sturdy and strong
He never grew cold although he lived very long.

His beak and his legs were as yellow as the gold it do shine
And his gub it could bore an inch hole in a very short time.

And I have travelled Killarney, Killgarven, Kanturk, and Millstreet
Along by Cork Harbour I'd be hawking in turkeys and in geese
But in all of my rambles and travels no finer did I meet
Than the likes of Bill's gander for grandeur and very fine breed

Now the girls they all came for game and they were looking for breed
When they heard of the name and the fame of Bill and his Geese
They measured this gander's fine legs with a carpenter's rule
But they never could part him once they saw the fine length of his wings.

There is a wit and a genius threaded through this song of internal rhyme and rhythm that is a quintessential Irish mix of the brilliant and the utterly absurd, the beautiful and the ridiculous. The song is about nothing and everything all at once. The genius is buried deep inside the nonsensical. I love it. My only great regret is that, like most great songs, we have absolutely no idea who wrote it. If I knew who the man was I would visit his grave every year and place goose feathers by his tombstone. May he rest always in peace for he has given me much.

Had I not wandered into that pub beside Grehan's on that Tuesday after the All Ireland Fleadh Cheoil in 1967 I would never have met Willie Clancy and I would never have learned 'The Gander' and my entire life would have been just that fraction less enriched. Chance is an extraordinary thing all the same, is it not?

Attending Fleadh Cheoils during the 1960s was a hazardous business and never quite risk free. First of all there were the messers and the cowboys to be contended with. These were kind of benign lager louts with guitars and bodhráns who roamed the streets in droves singing or rather shouting out some of the words of 'The Black Velvet Band' or 'The Shoals of Herring', it had to be a 'Clancy number'. They were usually naked from the waist up. You could only put up with so much of these gobshites. Where they were really annoying was when someone, maybe a child even, was playing or singing something sweet and delicate that the rest of us wanted to listen to. Although in actual fact I have never been in a fight in my life, fighting with some of these yobdaws was always on the cards.

Another hazard about going to a Fleadh was the weather. We never brought sleeping bags or tents or anything like that with us. We didn't own such luxuries in the first place and in any case we didn't see any need for them. 'Accommodation' at a Fleadh was the first hay barn you could find outside the town. You had to scout for these in the daylight and before you got too drunk. In theory the whole thing sounds lovely, romantic even – sleeping snuggled up in the sweet new-mown hay and the farmer's wife bringing you out a cup of tea in the morning and the cuckoo calling in the background. The reality of course was something totally different.

In a hay barn just outside Clones it is pissing rain outside and it is 8.30 in the morning. Most of us are nursing moderate to severe hangovers and are having a bit of a lie-in. Christy Moore, Frank and Donal Lunny, Peter Sheehy, Mick Bulfin and a whole lot more of us are holed up in this shed. The next thing, and all of a sudden, don't we hear this madman of a farmer and he ranting and raving down on the floor under us. Then he grabs up a hayfork and starts lunging at the haystack to see if he can dislodge a few bodies. 'Get to fuck out of my hay barn,' he roars. I never saw a group of fellows leave a hay barn so quickly in all my life, rain or no rain.

I remember another wet Fleadh Cheoil, this time in Thurles. The trouble here was that we had fallen into a serious session of music and singing early in the day and never got to scout for a hay barn. When the music and the drinking and the craic were all over we came out to find it dark and raining. This time it was every man for himself. Having wandered around for a while I eventually found a greyhound track with starting traps. I gladly climbed into one of these and, snug and out of the rain and the wind, I slept the sleep of the just. Hotels, guesthouses and even B&Bs were considered at the time to be a waste of good drinking money.

It was while playing and singing in O'Donoghue's of Merrion Row that I first met my wife to be, Ann Hughes. She and two of her girlfriends just wandered in there one evening and sat at the table around which we were playing. These three young women worked together in the blood bank and lived in a flat just up the road in Upper Leeson Street. They, each of them, seemed to have a love for and a grasp of the kind of music we were doing but no one more so than Ann. After the session I accompanied the three of them back to their flat where I was introduced to the as yet unfamiliar world of air hostesses and blood bank attendants. I had been spending too much time with musicians, bohemians and medical students. But here there was a whiff of glamour and a new world to be explored.

* * *

Running parallel to all the Dublin stuff we had, if you like, our country seat in the form of Pat Dowling's public house in Prosperous, county Kildare and the old kitchen in the basement of Downings House a mile away. The secret to the success of these twin institutions was their closeness to Dublin and the almost irresistible attraction that traditional musicians and singers had and still have for things rural. The roots of most folk music are sustained in the soil of the countryside and therefore frequent excursions out of the city become an imperative for anyone serious about playing, singing or just listening to this kind of music.

But why Prosperous you might reasonably ask. It could have been some place handier to the city like Lucan or Clonee or some place like that which in those days would still have qualified as 'the countryside'. The answer to this is, as so often is the case, people and circumstances. The people in question were my brother Davoc, his friend Ciarán Burke who was later to join The Dubliners, myself and Pat Dowling, the man himself who had at the time just bought the pub from the Cribbins.

Those were the people. The circumstances were that in early 1963 Davoc was doing up a cottage that he had beside the big house and, being a bit strapped for cash, he somehow prevailed on Ciarán Burke to lend a hand. Ciarán, with his then girlfriend, Jeanie Bonham, more or less encamped on site working on the cottage by day and drinking in Dowlings by night. To the people of Prosperous Ciarán and Jeanie would have cut quite an extraordinary dash. Had two aliens from Mars been thrown in their midst they could hardly have been any more different. They were in fact classic beatniks but the problem was that beatniks had not been invented yet so nobody knew what to call them or how to classify them. He was handsome and tall with a Parnell-like beard, tweed jacket and general unkempt appearance, she was small and squat in a floral dress, beads and bangles and smelling of smouldering sandalwood.

But it hardly mattered what they looked like. It was what they were able to do that mattered. Ciarán played a Clark's tin-whistle and kind of sang in a husky and slightly off-key voice. Jeanie was the better singer. They sang a duet thus:

> *Soldier, Soldier, Soldier, would you marry me now?*
> *With a hey and a ho and the sound of a drum.*
> *Arrah no fair maid I couldn't marry you.*
> *Because I have no shoes to put on.*
> *So she ran to the shop as fast as she could run*
> *With a hey and a ho and the sound of a drum*
> *And she brought him a pair of the very very best*
> *Saying here my small man put them on.*

And so on in that vein until your man has built up quite a good wardrobe for himself and never marries her in the end because as he says in the very last line of the song: 'I have my own wife at home.' Innocent stuff for sure but then these were innocent days. Ciarán would then encourage some local character like Larry Dowd or the Pike Keegan to sing a song and all of a sudden there was a proper session going, something very unusual for the days that were in it. Pat Dowling stayed quietly in the background but did everything in his power to encourage these sessions, firstly because he loved the craic but also because he could see the potential that singing and music sessions like these had as crowd pullers into his new pub.

Word quickly spread that there was some right good sport going on in Pat Dowling's pub. Soon local musicians, who up until then we didn't even know existed, started to drift in. People like Ned Farrell on the bodhrán and piper Mick Crehan from Naas who later was to play at the graveside when Willie Clancy died. There was box player Gerry O'Mahony and his wife, Peggy Carroll, who was a good singer. There was banjo player, Joe Ward; the Moran brothers, Denny and Ducks from Robertstown, both box players; Frank Burke from Sligo, fiddle player and singer; Mickey Maguire, flute player from Coill Dubh always with his wife, Mary, who could lilt a fine tune. Then there were the Newbridge brigade, Donal and Frank Lunny, often with their parents, Frank senior and Mary Lunny. Christy Moore and his mother, Nancy, and maybe his brothers, Barry and Andy, and later his sisters, Anne, Terry and Eilish, all good singers. Nan McCormack would try to organise us. There were various members of the soon to be defunct Liffey Folk Four. Within a few weeks a legend was born that was to last for the better part of the next ten years. These were the Wednesday night sessions in Dowlings of Prosperous.

Pat Dowling was a generous man. Singers and musicians would all be looked after with a free pint or two and towards the end of the evening a massive plate of sandwiches would somehow materialise, having been made up by Maureen in the back kitchen. Maureen was Mick Crehan's landlady and we were always trying to get her fixed up with Pat Dowling because neither of them was married and it seemed to us a good idea and a perfect match. The sandwiches were made with white batch loaf, roast beef and YR sauce, just the lad for hungry musicians. The musicians that I have mentioned here were, if you like, the core people. In addition to these we always had our Dublin contingent join in the sessions. I am not going to start naming all the famous and not so famous singers and musicians who would join us from time to time. Just take my word for it. There were very few singers or musicians indeed frequenting the pubs and clubs around Dublin during the 1960s who did not call into at least some of the Wednesday night sessions in Dowlings of Prosperous.

The second leg of this most extraordinary academy of Irish folk music was the old kitchen in the basement of the big house – Downings. When conditions were right or when the spirit moved us, or if there were some special people in for the session, perhaps no more than two or three times a year, all the musicians and singers and characters down in Dowlings would be issued with verbal invitations and asked to come on up to the house and we would keep the craic going. They had to bring their own drink and no food would be served. These parties were all about venue and music and if that was not enough for you then you knew where to go.

The basement had a hard-stone flagged floor, which lent the room fantastic natural acoustics and resonance. The uilleann piping of say Liam Óg Flynn or the mandolin playing of Francy Grehan were all greatly enhanced by this feature. Heat of a winter's night was provided for by way of an enormous open fire onto which old furniture was usually thrown – benches or old chests of drawers or anything that came to hand. Davoc was in the antique business at this stage so burning old furniture was not quite as bizarre as may first appear. And in any case it was always good for a laugh. There was a pair of hob-nailed boots kept on a shelf. If anyone was in the mood for it they could put these on and batter to the music. At times the whole place took on a surreal quality, an out of this world aura to it all.

And if you should go away across the ocean,
Then take me back you to be your servant,
In fare and in market you will me well looked after.
And you will sleep with a Greek king's daughter.

You took what's behind me and what's before me
You took east and west when you wouldn't mind me
The sun, moon and stars from my sky you have taken
And God as well or I am much mistaken.

CHAPTER 6

Making of a Doctor

All during these medical school years I would live at home in Downings House during the holidays and in flats or digs during term. In all I lived in no fewer than fourteen different addresses around Dublin as a medical student. I often shared places with my good friends Óg and his brother Peter Sheehy in Charleston Avenue near Ranelagh and later out in a flat in Fairview. Also I once shared a place in Rathmines with Tony McMahon, the great box player. Tony flew through pre-med in Surgeons and then seemed to lose interest in medicine having got over the biggest hurdle in the entire course. He once found me playing the tin-whistle during an idle moment and said that it was a horrible tune made worse by my playing of it. If you were looking for compliments then Tony would not be your first port of call. He was hugely intolerant of any player not up to his own very high standards. But once you got to know Tony you soon found out that his bark was worse than his bite.

A strange thing about going through the six-year course of medicine is that the longer you go on the easier it becomes. For example human anatomy is a horrible subject that requires you to submit reams upon reams of largely useless information into your brain and to regurgitate it at exam time. The next year or two are not much better. But when you come to the two final clinical years during which you study medicine, surgery, paediatrics, obstetrics and gynaecology, ophthalmology, some psychiatry, radiology and dermatology, all of these subjects are rational, practical, interesting, and easy to remember and to understand.

Practical medicine is taught at the bedside and we all flock around the poor patient up on Richmond One. The women are allowed up front because in the main they are not as tall as the fellows. Some of the fellows, but one in particular, seems to always get himself up right beside the patient. This guy pisses the rest of us off a bit. Professor Alan Thompson is giving the tutorial. The patient, an elderly man, is suffering from chronic bronchitis and emphysema or, as we would say nowadays, chronic obstructive airways disease or COAD for short. In hospital, as a kind of a code, they were often just referred to as 'blue puffers'. At that time hospital wards in Dublin were full of blue puffers whose conditions were exacerbated by the higher levels of air pollution that we had in those days. Blue puffers were considered good teaching material because they had a lot of signs and symptoms – a lot of things to 'demonstrate' as we used to say.

Even though we had two more years to go we were often, a bit sarcastically I suspect, addressed as doctor.

'Tell me, doctor,' says Professor Thompson, looking straight at me, 'What do you think is the matter with this poor man?' This is the first real live 'patient' that I have ever seen in my life and the professor wants an opinion from me! But to be fair about it Professor Thompson, who always wore a dickey bow and was the first radio doctor to ever broadcast on Radio Éireann, was a gentleman and a kind teacher. He saw my discomfort and offered me a way forward.

'Does the man look well or does he look ill?' he wanted to know.

And there was my very first lesson in clinical medicine and one that all doctors instinctively use throughout their professional lives. Simple commonsense, intelligent and straightforward observation can still tell you more about a person than even the most sophisticated blood test or scans. Does the person look well or ill? Always look your patient straight in the face and ask yourself that question.

'He looks very ill, sir,' I proffered. The professor concurred.

Someone suffering end stage 'cor pulmonale', as this condition is also sometimes referred to, looks dreadfully unwell. Their functioning lungs, which should look like a large bunch of tiny grapes, are now more like a bunch of tennis balls. Thus the surface area of the lungs used to oxygenate the blood and carry away carbon dioxide is massively reduced. The patient's lips are constantly blue, or cyanosed as we say in the trade, due to a chronic lack of oxygen and excess CO_2. In an effort to get as much air into their lungs as possible the patient holds his chest wall in the full inspiration or expanded position and this is referred to as 'barrel chested'. While breathing out the patient purses his lips in an effort to push back the escaping air so as to leech out of it the maximum possible amount of oxygen. When you look at their fingernails, blue puffers will often exhibit 'clubbing' a sure sign of long-term oxygen starvation. This man is slowly dying in front of us.

All of these things are carefully pointed out to us and their significance explained. This is part one of the steps to be taken in order to reach a diagnosis. It is referred to as 'inspection' and it is what you can see with your eyes before laying a hand on the patient. Auscultation comes next.

One of the greatest inventions ever made in medicine has to be the stethoscope. Simple and all as it may be, it has to remain up there with anaesthesia, x-rays, insulin, vaccines and penicillin. It was first devised by a French chest physician, Dr Rene Laennec, in 1816 as a simple cardboard, and later a wooden, tube. Indeed it was not until nearly the end of that century that the stethoscope began to take on its present form of two earpieces connected by tubing to a diaphragm.

Just as all anglers are said never to forget catching their first salmon, so too it can be said that all doctors remember purchasing their first stethoscope. This is a ritual before entering your second last year of medicine. Mine was proudly bought in Fannin's of Grafton Street. The trick then was to carry it around in your pocket with part of it sticking out for all to see. A stethoscope is as iconic to a doctor as a whistle is to a referee or a crozier to a bishop; the only difference being that the former two may be of some practical use while the latter is of none.

When growing up as a child I always thought that there was

something terribly clever about the way a doctor could place the bell of a stethoscope on your back, ask you to breathe in and out and that this actually told the doctor something about what was going on inside you. But actually there really is not all that much to it once you have a bit of practice. We line up to listen to this poor man's lungs. Professor Thompson tells us where to place the stethoscope and then asks us to describe what we are hearing. We already know what a normal lung should sound like because earlier several of us had taken our shirts off and allowed our colleagues to listen to our healthy young lungs. Listening to a normal healthy lung through a stethoscope you hear a sound like a gentle breeze through the trees. But when you listen to this poor man's lungs there is no breeze at all, there is at first a hideous silence. And then, like a cry in the night, you hear something that just sounds all wrong, something foreign and strange to nature. We call these 'rals' in the trade. They are a kind of a musical liquid clicking sound, the sound of air travelling through disease. The sound of approaching death.

On another ward a young woman has pneumonia. These days you would not routinely hospitalise someone with this condition but forty years ago doctors were more conservative. The professor asks the lady if she would mind if all ten of us took turns to listen to her lungs. She seems quite happy to oblige. People, God bless them all, seem to understand that medical students have got to learn somewhere and are generally happy to lend a hand.

When you listen with a stethoscope to the lungs of someone with lobar pneumonia you hear the sound of a gentle breeze through the trees throughout the lungs until you come to the part that is infected. At this precise point you hear something totally different and strange. In the trade we call these sounds 'crepitations', classically likened to the sound of snow being crushed under foot as you walk along of a winter's evening. But this group of students has a problem with that description, accurate and all as it may be. They all come from countries where it never snows so they have no idea what we are talking about. Someone produces a balloon and blows it up. If you rub the surface of an inflated balloon you can produce a sound exactly like the crepitations of pneumonia. We are all learning fast.

In the afternoon it is surgery with Professor William McGowan upstairs on Richmond Four. A fifteen-year-old girl has been admitted with abdominal pain and vomiting. Again it is inspection first. Just look at the abdomen and see if you notice anything strange. Usually you won't but in rare circumstances like bowel obstruction you may see what's called 'visible peristalsis' or forceful movements in the bowel against the obstruction. One or two of us only then are asked to palpate her abdomen. The other students will have to wait for another day but all of this stuff is vitally important and critical to the making of a competent doctor.

First you ask the patient to point with one finger to where the pain is. Later when the students have turned into doctors and have gained experience they will learn that in practice, in the case of very small children, when you ask them to point to the pain, the mother often steps in and tries to do it for the child. I know the mother means well but this is a big mistake. The child knows exactly where the pain is. And besides children are honest and have no hidden agenda like trying to justify their concerns or justify their presence in your surgery.

You palpate an abdomen gently but firmly using the tips of your fingers with the palm of your hand spread out and laid on the skin. Watch the patient's face, not your hand and start at the point furthest away from the pain. You do not prod or poke and you are ever mindful of the structures underneath where you are feeling. When you come to the point where the patient indicated the pain to be at its worst, you may or may not elicit tenderness and cause the patient to grimace or the child to cry. At this point too there may be muscle guarding or tightening of the abdominal muscles protecting the source of the pain. If you do all this correctly then you may never miss the diagnosis of appendicitis. But there isn't a doctor that I know, including myself, who could honestly claim any such record.

* * *

It was during these final two clinical years at the College of Surgeons in Dublin that I developed a love for game shooting – a hobby that would eventually surpass, though never replace, my interests in Irish music and singing. Shooting is an interest that I carried through all of my life. In these parts the sport can be divided roughly into three divisions – rough shooting, driven shooting and wildfowling or duck shooting. Rough shooting in turn can be divided into two groups – snipe and woodcock shooting or rough shooting pheasants. At this stage, when I was in my final medical school years, I really only knew about rough shooting pheasants. Woodcock and snipe, wildfowling, driven shooting and clay pigeon were all to come later.

There are two ways of rough shooting pheasants. You can use springer spaniels and run them along the hedges and ditches and through the stubble and root crops, all the time hoping that they will come on pheasant and flush them within range for you. The problem with this approach is that spaniels, other than the exceptional field trial specialists, tend to go like hell and there is always the danger that when they do put up birds that these will be out of range of the guns. Birds were too scarce to be flushing wild when I did my early shooting.

The other way to rough shoot pheasants is to use pointers or setters or, as our ghillie down in Kerry, Eugene Hayes, calls them, 'stopping dogs'. My friend Joe Ward outside Prosperous kept shorthaired liver and white English pointers and these were perfect for the kind of terrain that we were shooting over – a mixture of cutaway bog and agricultural land. The great thing about shooting over pointers is the comfort that's in it. When a pointer gets a whiff of a pheasant he freezes immediately like a piece of sculpture. You know that there is a bird around somewhere. But you do not know exactly where it is or when it will burst onto wing and take off rocketing across the ditch.

In the two seasons that I shot with Joe Ward and his pointers I do not believe that I shot one single pheasant. I did not know how to shoot in those days and it was not until I got lessons in clay shooting in Canada a few years later that I began to understand what was involved. But Joe was a generous man and would always give me a bird or two to take home and no one was any the wiser and everyone thought that I could shoot.

But the point of shooting, strangely, is not about killing birds. It is mainly the working and watching of the dogs, not the actual shooting itself, that makes this sport so enjoyable. When I think back on those wintry Sundays and Joe Ward and I out under clear blue skies very early on a frosty morning, in and around the Cot bog or Ballinafagh or Kilmurray where the rushes might be frozen solid and the gorse still showing an occasional golden bloom, or where the hawthorns had not even yet dropped the last of its dark red berries and blackbirds cry in alarm in front of our stopping dogs, when I recall all of this, as I often do, I am again filled with a warm and good feeling and I know that life for the most part is wonderful.

* * *

Now my mother is writing her biography of Francis Ledwidge, the pastoral poet who lived just outside Slane in county Meath. This is a fairly massive undertaking involving all new research and interviewing no fewer than thirty of the poet's own contemporaries still alive at the time. The entire work takes her eight years to complete – from 1964 to 1972 – during which time her health was to deteriorate quite markedly. The reasons why my mother undertook such a labour of love were, I think, threefold:

Firstly Cardinal Wright of Boston, with whom she enjoyed a warm friendship over her many years lecturing in the United States, suggested the idea for this biography to her.

Secondly there was the question of her own brother Richard who was a private in the Irish Guards and killed in the Battle of the Somme on 15 September 1916. Ten months later on 31 July 1917 Francis Ledwidge was blown to pieces and died instantly when a stray shell exploded beside him as he worked at road building behind the battle lines of Ypres in Belgium near the French border.

And thirdly, and perhaps most compelling of all, it was there to be done. Nobody had thought to capture this gentle poet's short life in a biography until my mother saw fit to do so. She most certainly did not do it for the money. She worked on the book over a period of eight years and received total royalties of only £200.

As a literal artist of the Irish Renaissance of the early part of the twentieth century, Ledwidge did, or certainly was destined to had his life not been cut so short, rank with the best of them; with Yeats, Kavanagh, Russell and Colum. The wonder then is not that my mother should have taken up the challenge when she did; the real wonder is that nobody seems to have done so many years earlier.

Thomas MacDonagh, executed at Arbour Hill following the 1916 Easter Rising, was one of Francis Ledwidge's best friends and his mentor. They were, after all, fellow poets and nationalists. One of MacDonagh's main interests and talents was the translating of early bardic poems from Irish into English in a manner that preserved the rhythm and internal rhyming system unique to this period. Cathal Buí Mac Giolla Ghunna was such a bardic poet and coming upon a dead bittern on his journeys wrote his well-known poem 'An Bonnan Buí' or in English 'The Yellow Bittern'. MacDonagh translated the first verse thus:

> Oh yellow bittern who never broke out
> On a drinking bout may as well have drunk.
> For his bones are now thrown on a naked stone
> Where he lived alone like a hermit monk.
> And had I known you were so near your death
> Or had my breath held out I'd have run to you
> Till a splash from the lake of the sons of all birds
> Would have stirred your heart to life anew.

When Francis Ledwidge heard of the execution of his great friend Thomas MacDonagh he must have felt torn with bitter sadness, great anger, resentment and confusion. Crown forces, the same crown forces for whom Ledwidge was then fighting, had executed his best friend. The Meath poet was on leave back home in Ireland in the weeks following the rising and MacDonagh's execution. Returning to the front lines to fight on the side of those who had executed his great friend must have been nigh on impossible. Echoing the resonances in his friend's poem 'The Yellow Bittern' Ledwidge wrote of his executed friend:

> He shall not hear the bittern cry
> In the wide sky, where he is lain,
> Nor voices of the sweeter birds
> Above the wailing of the rain.
>
> Nor shall he know when loud March blows,
> Through slanting snows her fanfare shrill,
> Blowing to flame the golden cup
> Of many an upset daffodil.
>
> But when the dark cow leaves the moor,
> And pastures poor with greedy weeds,
> Perhaps he'll hear her low at morn
> Lifting her horn in pleasant meads.

During the Irish folk revival of the mid-1960s, and completely independent of the fact that my mother was at the time researching Ledwidge and MacDonagh, I had actually learned the English or MacDonagh version of 'An Bonnan Buí' and had been singing it at the various gigs around Dublin at the time. When my mother discovered this she was absolutely bowled over by the serendipity of it all. To her dying day this song remained her favourite and she would ask me to sing it for her on any old pretext or occasion.

* * *

It was in the winter of 1966 that Christy Moore did me a good turn. I never actually asked him to do it but of his own volition he got me a series of gigs over a two-week period in and around the folk clubs of Manchester and Birmingham where he was well got at the time. At this stage Christy's own career had not yet taken off nor could either of us at that time have anticipated just how enormously successful he would become some ten or fifteen years later. We were staying with a relation of Christy's who ran a vegetable shop and she kind of mothered us and kept an eye on us, for mothering we badly needed. I remember I had a woeful hangover one day and I got into a box of grapefruits from the shop below and ate them one after another. Grapefruits are a great cure for a hangover.

While thus recovering on a bed upstairs Christy thought that I could be better engaged and set me up in front of a tape recorder and asked that I sing some of my better songs into it because he wanted to learn some of them, not indeed that he was in any way stuck for material himself. I sang 'The Cliffs of Duneen', 'Who are you my Pretty Fair Maid?', 'My Dark-Eyed Sailor' and 'The Banks of the Lee'. The last song there has nothing to do with the other 'The Banks' as usually sung around Cork but goes:

> When two lovers meet down beneath the green bower
> When two lovers meet down beneath the green tree
> Where Mary, fond Mary, she declared unto her lover
> You have stolen away my young heart from the banks of the Lee.

This short singing tour was otherwise a great success. The folk clubs paid generously so I came home a lot better off than when I left. In time Christy started to include all the songs that I gave him into his repertoire. In fact two of them are on the very successful *Prosperous* album and Christy generously acknowledges this on the record sleeve. The *Prosperous* record, recorded in the basement of this house here, was the precursor and catchiest for the group Planxty. Any time that he sings any of 'my songs' Christy in fairness to him always acknowledges their source.

* * *

The second last summer before my final year at Surgeons I spent in Naas Hospital under the guidance of county surgeon Jack Gibson. Jack was famous as a hypnotist and would sometimes attempt to operate on people using only hypnosis and no anaesthesia. I have to say that this did not impress me one little bit. I believe in the powers of suggestion and therefore in the curative potential of hypnosis which, at the end of the day, is really only a strong form of suggestion. But to extend this potential to blocking out the pain of surgery would require an exceptionally skilled therapist working with an exceptionally suggestible patient. Jack Gibson may not have had this skill because some of the patients that I saw being operated on and who were supposedly 'under hypnosis' were in fact wide-awake and suffering.

When I'd come home from working in Naas Hospital in the evenings my brother would complain that I washed my hands like a doctor and worse still I smelled like a doctor. I am not sure what washing one's hands like a doctor means but the reason I smelled like a doctor was because even then they were still using ether as an anaesthetic in Naas. Sometimes I'd be called upon to administer the ether drop by drop onto a gauze held over the patient's mouth and nose. Ether was and indeed still is a very safe and effective general anaesthetic. One of the minor problems about using it is that it stinks the whole place out and that the person administering it also cannot avoid inhaling some of the stuff and reeking of it afterwards. But there are worse smells than ether.

The final year is spent living in hospitals, the so-called 'residency year'. First I am billeted in the Rotunda Maternity Hospital and later in the Richmond Hospital, both institutions being on the northside of Dublin. Obstetrics, at least in theory, is an easy and logical subject. It is also an extremely hazardous one where there are always two people's lives, health and well-being at risk. The word obstetrics comes from the Latin *ob*, to stand by or to stare, which is very interesting given that modern obstetrics is the exact antithesis of that and is all about interfering and intervening. For example the Caesarean section rate in most maternity hospitals nowadays would be about twenty per cent, the induction rate would be similar at around twenty per cent while the episiotomies and forceps delivery rate might be as high as forty per cent. In effect nowadays most women entering a maternity hospital to give birth can expect some intervention or other. Totally natural birth in a maternity hospital is the exception rather than the rule. If a woman wants to be assured that there will be no unnecessary meddling while she gives birth then the only way is to arrange for a home birth, a practice frowned upon by maternity hospitals who do not like the notion of any competition. This is a controversy in which I was to become embroiled later in life.

There is a saying in obstetrics with respect to childbirth that all medical students should 'see one, do one and teach one' and that is more or less what we did. In practice in those days competent, if not very sympathetic, midwifery nurses conducted most deliveries and we students were only in the way most of the time. But we did need some hands-on experience and all of us would have 'delivered' at least one baby during our 'midder' stint. This for the most part meant controlling the baby's head as it emerged through the vulva and then lifting the baby out and cutting and tying the umbilical cord – not much to it really provided of course that there were no complications.

We sat around in the tea-room all day smoking cigarettes or in my case a pipe, playing poker and waiting for the alarm bell to go. The alarm bell signalled that a complicated delivery was imminent and that we needed to go at once to the delivery ward to see what was going on. Complications in the main were multiple or twin births; mal-presentation, as for example a breech delivery where the baby comes out bum first; and prolapsed cord, which is a very dangerous situation for the baby. In any of these situations the consultant obstetrician would often exhibit life-saving skills and the whole justification for their existence became quite obvious.

There was a man in our class by the name of Jimmy Martin. Jimmy was a self-made man in that before he could enter medical school he had to do the leaving certificate as an adult by attending night classes, while during the day he ran a small supermarket on Lower Rathmines Road. His dream and one ambition was to become a doctor and he would often say things like: 'Just imagine lads, in two years' time we will all be doctors and earning good money and we will be out on the golf course twice a week and leading the good life.'

I do not know where poor Jimmy got his false vision of what doctoring is all about but he died only a few years after qualifying – perhaps from disappointment and disillusionment. But he was an amusing and droll Dub. When my turn came to deliver my first baby Jimmy was at the looking-on stage. After the delivery he and I went across the road to Mooney's for a pint where student and obstetricians alike were wont to frequent. As we sipped our pints of Guinness Jimmy said to me: 'Jasus, Andy I loved the way you delivered that baby. I particularly like the way you caught it as it flew by.' This of course was a rather irreverent reference to the fact that many of the women delivering babies in the Rotunda in those days were 'gran-multips' meaning in plain English that they had given birth to five or more babies already. As such then their deliveries were often, thought not always of course, quick and uncomplicated affairs where the baby arrived without the need of even minimal intervention.

After three months' residency in obstetrics it was off to the Richmond Hospital to gain some in-house experience in medicine and surgery. Here we slept in dormitories divided into rather primitive cubicles and we drank around the corner in Church Street if I was not otherwise engaged with music or ballads. In this place too we played poker deep into the night – five cards and seven cards 'stud poker' where the stakes were high and the incidence of bluffing even higher. Bringing girlfriends into this sanctuary was allowed but not encouraged. One night my girlfriend and I stole the bed of a colleague who was on night duty. As a precaution against interruption we pushed a wardrobe across the door, which was at the bottom of the bed. Sometime in the middle of the night my colleague came off duty and not unreasonably went looking for his bed back. In pushing his way into the cubical he pushed the wardrobe right on top of us and then proceeded to climb over the back of it in order to communicate his desire to retrieve his bed. So there we all were, girlfriend and I on the bottom, the wardrobe on top of us and finally my displaced colleague on top of that and he giving out yards.

Final exams were taken in two phases. At Christmas during the fifth and final medical year we did our so-called 'smalls', which consisted of paediatrics, psychiatry, ophthalmology and ear nose and throat surgery. The following June we took our medical, surgical, obstetrical and gynaecological practical and written examinations. I passed the lot of them first attempt, not with any particular distinction it must be said but a pass is a pass and with something approaching ease I became a doctor at long last.

Graduation day is one that no doctor ever forgets. It's been such a long, long haul. Two years trying to get through pre-med were followed by five intensive years first of anatomy and physiology and then pathology and pharmacology and finally paediatrics, obstetrics, gynaecology, medicine and surgery. Throughout most of these years I consider myself extremely lucky to have been able to find some paid work through singing and playing the tin-whistle. Not only did the money come in very handy but also the diversion away from medical school was therapeutic and afforded a better-balanced view of things. Graduation is at least the end of the beginning. On this happy day you recite the Hippocratic oath and collect your certificates upstairs in the elegant banquet hall. Afterwards we all had planned to get drunk in Rice's pub down the street. We met there all right but after three or four pints the notion of actually getting drunk did not appeal and we dispersed happily.

Now is the time for some serious decision-making. Six weeks before graduation Ann and I marry in the church in Haddington Road. There is a child on the way. There are serious times ahead for all of us and nothing had better go wrong.

CHAPTER 7

Canada

After graduation from medical school one has a number of critical choices to make, all of which will have life-long consequences. Like most of my colleagues I had more or less made up my mind what way I was going to go long before I graduated. First of all there is the question of internship. One year working in a teaching hospital is mandatory for all medical graduates before they are fully registered as doctors. Before that, registration is only provisional or temporary. So the first question is, where will you do your internship year, in Ireland or abroad? The next question is what do you want to do after internship? Do you want to become a general practitioner or some kind of hospital consultant? If you want to become a consultant you need to start lining yourself in one particular direction, if a general practitioner, in a different direction.

I found these decisions very easy to reach. Quite frankly I had had enough of medical school and lectures and ward rounds and exams and autopsies and living from hand to mouth and borrowing money and being a burden on my poor parents. I was twenty-six years of age, newly married to Ann Hughes and our first child was on its way. I wanted to do general practice and Canada was full of opportunities in this regard, offering rotating internships specifically designed for that discipline. Everything medical in Ireland was a struggle in the late 1960s. There were too many doctors and competition for places in practice or in training was fierce. And in any case there is a long history in Irish medicine of doctors going abroad for a few years before settling back home. Travelling broadens the mind they say and going to Canada for internship and a few years general practice may have been among the best decisions of my life although at first it may not have seemed that way.

Hamilton, Ontario, where we were to spend the next year of our lives cooped up in a hospital apartment is, or certainly was, a singularly uninspiring polluted industrial city, nestled, if that is the right word, on the shores of Lake Ontario. If you were stupid enough, as we were, to go sunbathing in Hamilton you ended up covered in tiny iron filings. You wouldn't get a tan at all; it would be more like a sheen. Brendan Behan is accredited with saying of Hamilton, Ontario: 'I could not be blasphemous enough about that place.' This outburst is thought to have been inspired by Brendan's failure to locate any kind of alcoholic beverage in the city on a Sunday when he arrived there, a bitter disappointment that we were to share with Behan on our arrival in that God-forsaken place.

Canada, or certainly Ontario, had the most restrictive drinking laws at that time. There were no pubs at all, none whatsoever. If you had to drink, and certainly there was very little encouragement for you to do so, then you had to go to a licensed government-run 'beer store' to get beer or cider or lager or drinks of that kind. If you wanted spirits like whiskey or gin or vodka or if you wanted wine, you had to go to another government-run 'liquor store'. These two kinds of controlled outlets were never in one and the same place, nor for that matter were they ever even remotely adjacent to each other. They closed all day Sunday so the Sabbath was strictly observed. You had to sign a form saying how much alcohol you had purchased and everything was made as unpleasant and as difficult as possible for you to get a few drinks for your fridge. It was all a big deal and a guilt-ridden operation.

Here we were, two young people, graduates of one of the liveliest pub cultures in the world and suddenly we find ourselves in this Canadian industrial wasteland. No pubs, no singing, no music, no craic. But help was to be at hand. There were other Irish in town and there had been other Irish in town for generations and they, just like we were feeling now, had missed the good social life of back home. Under the inspiration and leadership of one Pat Cassidy and one John Roach in 1952 they formed the Irish Canadian Club up on the escarpment overlooking the city. I can honestly say that it was this Irish Canadian Club that, more than anything else, eased our way into life in Canada and helped us retain some degree of sanity and balance. Normally I would steer clear of my countrymen when abroad. For example if in Madrid or Rome or Boston I would not dream of going into an 'Irish pub' but would rather give them a wide berth. But this was different and we were hungry for something approaching normality and Irishness.

Every Friday night this place would come alive with songs and dance and music and general craic. We made some great friends with fellow musicians and singers like Chris and Peggy Jones, Raymond Reynolds and Loo Crowe from Dublin, and Tommy and Nelly Curran from Carlow. While the majority of club members were southern Irish Catholics with their Canadian husbands or wives, there were a small but significant number of northerners there too, though of what persuasion we never knew nor asked nor did it seem to matter one iota. Whether nationalist or unionist they all pitched in and contributed to the general enjoyment of the place. We sang and played Irish and Canadian folk songs and music, Nova Scotia and Newfoundland being the source for most of the Canadian stuff. Peggy sang:

Fare well to Nova Scotia
The sea bound coast.
Let your mountains dark and dreary be.
For when I'm far away
On the briny ocean tossed
Would you ever heave a sigh or a wish for me?

Most Canadian folk songs have a nautical twist to them while most of their music has an unmistakable Irish or Scottish feel to it.

Hamilton, with its population of some half a million people, had large communities of various nationalities including an Italian-speaking district, a Polish-speaking district and a German-only region. Each of these regions would have had ethnic markets selling foods germane to the country in question. But the overall feel and ethos of the city was WASP or White Anglo-Saxon Protestant whose seriously boring and killjoy attitudes seem to hold sway; hence no drink available anywhere on Sundays. Down in the interns' lounge we had a soft drinks machine converted into a bottled beer dispenser and so we were able to beat the system to some small extent.

There were two linked hospitals – Hamilton General Hospital where we lived beside the Stelco steelworks and where the air was pretty foul, and the Nora Henderson Hospital up on the mountain where the air was fresher and a bit cooler. I chose a rotating internship with two months each in paediatrics, surgery, medicine, ears nose and throat, obstetrics and finally accident and emergency where drunken Indians plagued us all night long. These hospitals were affiliated to McMaster University faculty of medicine, the first medical school in the world to recognise general practice as a specialty in its own right. There was a lot of serendipity in all of this but as it happens the teaching was good and the orientation towards my chosen field of general practice could hardly have been better.

That autumn of 1968 our son Lorcan was born. Life takes on a more serious hue and things are never quite the same again. Because I must carry on my responsibilities as an intern I am somehow torn between the worries associated with new parenthood and those of career. I have a sense of unhappiness emanating from my wife Ann who I think now feels somewhat trapped and discontented. These feelings of ours may be the very beginnings of a marital disharmony that would eventually engulf us. Travelling up to the Nora Henderson Hospital in my open-topped, yellow MGB a song is playing on the radio with the words 'Such are the dreams of the everyday housewife'. I do not know what in fact were supposed to be the dreams of the everyday housewife. But it was the whole concept of her being described as everyday that I found very depressing and this somehow found resonance in my worrying marriage. I do not think that either of us was really ready for the permanent roles we were now going to have to play.

* * *

Winter is setting in and we are all a bit homesick. There are twenty-two of us interns, twenty men and only two women which even for that time was a disproportionate gender mix. Today the women would outnumber the men two to one. This is a diverse group of young doctors from all over the world with David Lintern and I being the only Dublin graduates in the place. David bought a black and white TV and after one week brought it back to the shop complaining that there were too many advertisements on it and that he no longer wanted it. And the strangest thing was the shop gave him a full refund with no quibbles. His wife Margaret was a great source of comfort and strength to Ann when Lorcan was born.

Downstairs in the interns' lounge was a big board with notices of all sorts pinned on to it. Most of these were to do with vacancies for doctors needed to work in hospitals or in general practice. At any given time there would be fifteen or twenty such notices pinned onto this although as the intern year started to draw to a close the number of notices started to increase. During my last month of internship there were at least six 'general practices for sale' posted up on this board. It really was just a question of where you wanted to go, city or country, small town or big town. The world was at our feet. The further from a major centre you chose, the cheaper the practice was to buy. One in particular caught my eye: Dr Jim Town with a growing practice in a place called Mitchell, Ontario wanted out and was giving the practice away for a nominal charge to cover instruments and equipment. I phoned Dr Town, told him I might be interested and arranged to meet him.

There was a certain method to this madness of choosing to go into the boondocks to take on a general practice when equally I could have chosen a nice university city like Toronto up the road or even nicer still, London, Ontario, 200 miles down the road, or Stratford, Ontario, just ten miles from Mitchell. In any of these places we would have had theatres, cinemas, good restaurants and so on. But I deliberately chose some place less attractive because I did not want to get caught, I did not want to get sucked into a system that might have made it difficult or nearly impossible to pull up roots and come back to Ireland after four or five years. For that was our aim and on that we kept focused.

Many doctors, now as then, leave Ireland for 'a few years' with the genuine expectation and plan of returning home after five years or so. But some never come home and end up spending the rest of their lives in exile in the UK, in America or Canada. We knew dozens of Irish doctors like that and I always thought there was something very sad about them and we were determined that this was not going to happen to us. What would happen is that they would set themselves up in practice in some fairly smart location, start making decent money, build a swimming pool and a tennis court and start living the so-called 'good life'. The next thing their children start going to school and making their own friends and before they know it the prospect of returning home to Ireland and starting all over again simply does not appeal. This is human but it is also sad.

Maybe I am reading this all wrong but when I heard doctors like that say how wonderful their lives in self-imposed exile were and what a good 'choice' they thought they had made and how happy the children were and so and so forth like that, I always felt that they were deluding themselves and were in denial. I found their attitudes to be more defensive than sincere and expressed with hidden sadness. Because at the end of the day the song is right, there is no place like home and there is no place like the country you were born and reared in, whatever its inadequacies may be. But perhaps not everyone shares that feeling as strongly as I do. Be that as it may we were quite determined not to make things too cushy for ourselves so taking up roots again would be no real hardship.

We chose well. In those days Mitchell, Ontario was sleepy, drab and dreary. With its population of some 2,000 souls this place just sat there with one road going into it and one road going out of it. All on the flat, some aspects of this little town, with its many wooden facades, bore some resemblance to a studio set for a Hollywood western. At any moment now the doors of the Grand Hotel will burst open and there will be a shoot-out between the good guys and the baddies.

There were no fewer than eight churches in Mitchell, each with its own small congregation. These were: First Lutheran Church, Free Reform Church, Grace Lutheran Church, Jehovah's Witnesses Kingdom Hall, Knox Presbyterian Church, St Vincent de Paul Catholic Church, Trinity Anglican Church and United Church. That's a lot of churches for a community of 2,000 people which I think speaks for itself. This is almost 'Bible Belt' stuff. Mitchell, like practically all small rural farming communities right across Ontario was populated largely by 'good God-fearing people'. The problem for us was that they were too good and too God-fearing for our taste. But there was no going back now and we would just have to see if we could root out some people with a bit of go and a bit of spice to them, not afraid to have a drink or to sing a song or play a tune or to curse a little or tell a dodgy story. Or in other words we were looking for real people, fallible, venial and slightly profane people. We needed to avoid serious Church-going teetotallers if we were to survive in these backwaters.

Another problem with living in such remoteness was that very many people in this area were not well-travelled and not well-read and seemed to have little interest in or knowledge of the greater world beyond their own boundaries. Good debate or intelligent discussion was therefore very hard to find. Of course one has to appreciate that these people were in the main second- and third-generation descendants from the original settlers. That if you like was their culture and as such was interesting in itself. But it took an awfully long time for it to sink into my head that 'culture' is not just about music and language and so on. Descendents from settlers also have a story to tell and a culture to be respected.

The winters were long and hard. It started to snow sometime in October and there was snow on the ground every day from then on through to mid-April or so. In the evenings most people stayed at home and watched ice hockey or curling on their TVs. The roads were kept passable most of the time through a system of routine snowploughing, salting and gritting. During particularly bad blizzards things might get out of control and there would be a few days every winter when roads became impassable and everything closed down. At times like these snow-machines or 'Skidoos' became the only mode of transport.

One such blizzard occurred in the early winter of 1972. At around midnight I received a phone call to tell me that there was a woman in labour at a farm outside of Monkton, about ten miles away. I was also advised that the local snowmobile club was on its way to pick me up and take me out there. This is a journey that will stay with me to the end of my days. I am in a caboose or sleigh hitched to the back of this very strong snowmobile holding onto my doctor's bag and peering out from time to time to see how we are going. I can only marvel at the bravery of these two men, one guiding us and the other towing me along. Our speed is perhaps fifteen miles an hour. The temperature is thirty degrees below. We are heading into a frozen abyss. Nothing makes sense and the full moon gives us light. Only the tips of the telephone posts and some telephone cable give us a clue as to where the roads might be twelve feet below us. This is unreal.

Eventually and by some miracle we arrive at this farmhouse to be greeted by a very relieved farmer. Upstairs I find his wife in the throes of labour. The baby's head is crowning and all is well. Like the good obstetrician that I am I stand idly by and do nothing other than mumble a few words of encouragement and allow nature to take its course. In a few minutes a fine baby boy is born and I cut the umbilical cord and deliver the placenta. Downstairs the men drink tea. I deliver the glad tidings from the bedroom upstairs and ask for a whiskey. There is none in the house. These people are after all 'good and God-fearing' and have no use for alcohol.

* * *

Men have just landed on the moon and it is a large general practice that I have inherited from my colleague, Jim Town, and it grows larger by the day. But I am young, enthusiastic and energetic. By the time I am ready to leave Mitchell and return home to Ireland for good this practice will have grown to twice its original size and number about 5,000 people. That in today's terms is a very large single-handed general practice. Age-wise it is an 'old' practice with the majority of patients being over fifty years of age. There are young women and their babies too, of course, but Mitchell is not the kind of place that would attract a lot of new residents, so the age profile of the practice was of necessity older. There is only one other doctor in town, Dr Prithem, and he is in his seventies and does no house calls or after-hours work. To my shame I never met Dr Prithem nor shook his hand. There was a chiropractor in town as well and he did a roaring trade. The competition for patients was, if you like, non-existent. I was seeing up to seventy patients per day, which was a huge workload. All patient visits were paid for by a state insurance scheme on a fee per item of service basis. There was no private practice as such. The fee was commensurate with the service given. You got paid so much for a consultation, so much for suturing a laceration, so much for carrying out a pap smear, syringing ears or setting a fracture. Practice was varied, interesting and very lucrative.

Mornings were spent at the local hospitals where all general practitioners had admitting rights and were expected to visit and care for their own patients, only seeking specialist consultation where necessary. We also delivered our own patients' babies, assisted at surgery and performed minor surgical procedures like tonsillectomies and vasectomies. At first I used a hospital in a place called Seaford, ten miles north-west of Mitchell, but there was a lot of squabbling going on there between the GPs and the one consultant surgeon who happened to be Nigerian. The arguments and disagreements were ostensibly to do with who should or could do what surgical procedure but I suspected that there was a good deal of racist overtones as well. I soon tired of this unpleasantness and switched my allegiance to a bigger and much better place – Stratford general hospital about ten miles south-east of Mitchell. Here they had several consultants in all the major surgical and medical fields and the atmosphere was convivial and pleasant. Hospital practice was always a learning experience and I could never understand why GPs in

Ireland are excluded from hospital practice and why they so meekly put up with the situation. When I returned to Ireland I greatly missed a hospital dimension to general practice but could raise no support among my colleagues for any changes to the status quo.

* * *

I did my first ten vasectomies in Seaford Hospital with the patient under general anaesthetic and GP Dr Paul Brady showing me what to do as best he could. You could never teach someone how to do a vasectomy other than if the patient is asleep. Imagine the anxiety you would cause a man if you tried to teach someone how to do a vasectomy on him while he was awake and listening to you tell your student to cut this and inject that. I know some of my colleagues disagree with me on this point but I believe that there's a limit as to what can and cannot be taught using a live and awake person as teaching material and that limit is surely vasectomy.

I say Paul Brady was doing his best to show me how to do a vasectomy because at the end of the day the operation is an entirely tactile one. It is all about feel and touch and not about seeing as is usually the case in surgery. If right-handed you retract the testicle gently with your right hand and gently palpate the contents of the spermatic cord with your left thumb below and your index and middle finger above. You know you have found the vas by the feel of it. *Gray's Anatomy* describes it as feeling like a 'whip cord' but since very few of us these days know what a whip cord is, never mind what it feels like, Gray's description is not much good to us. I describe it as feeling like, and being about the size of, a very undercooked piece of spaghetti. But there is no mistaking it. You either have it or you have not got it. It is never a maybe. Once you can routinely and quickly isolate the vas and anchor it between thumb below and index and middle finger above then you can do a vasectomy because the rest is relatively easy.

It took me about fifty vasectomies before I was confident enough to be able to carry on doing them without needing someone at hand to step in for me should I get into difficulty. Before I returned from Canada to Ireland I had done about one hundred vasectomies, all under local anaesthetic. I did vasectomies in Canada for the same reason that I did tonsillectomies – GP were expected to be able to do that kind of thing there. I had absolutely no idea at the time that vasectomy was to play such a major role in my life when I returned to Ireland a few years later. It simply did not occur to me that one day I might be the first Irish doctor to perform a vasectomy in Ireland.

To support a practice of the size that I had in Mitchell required that I employ two full-time secretaries and a full-time nurse. I had five inter-connecting examining-rooms and the nurse would always be one room ahead of me preparing a patient for examination or giving a vaccination or weighing a patient or taking their blood pressure or undressing a baby and generally smoothing the way for me so that my time with the patient could be focused and as brief as possible. My nurse, Anne Rowland, made life so much easier for both patient and doctor. We worked well as a team.

One day old Ned Horan came in to see me. Ned had Parkinson's disease and was generally bothered and hard of hearing. 'Ned, please take your shirt off and hang it in this closet here and I will be back to see you in a few minutes,' I said in my usual breezy way pointing out the closet to him and off I go to see another patient while Ned is getting ready.

After about ten minutes I go back to the room where I thought I had left Ned Horan and there is no sign of him. 'Where in the name of God has Ned taken himself to?' I ask myself, worried that he has wandered off into another examining-room and caused no end of consternation and embarrassment. Then I spotted it. Down at the bottom of the closet there is the toe of a boot sticking out. My next thought is that he has gone and hung himself – stranger things have happened in doctors' surgeries (or offices as we called them in Canada). I rushed over to the closet and flung the door open and there is poor old Ned Horan and he holding on to the coat hook at the back of the press for his dear life.

'What in the name of Jesus are you doing in there, Ned and will you come out of that at once?' I said to him more relieved than cross.

His answer was a classic: 'I'm doing the best I can doctor,' says he, implying that it was my fault that he was in there in the first place. When I asked Ned to hang his shirt in the closet he, being as deaf as a post, thought that I had asked him to hang onto the coat hook himself at the back of the closet and, thinking this to be some kind of new treatment as it were, he complied and in his own words did the best he could. Isn't it quite extraordinary what people used to do if a doctor advised it? I will tell you one thing, that day is long gone and maybe it's just as well.

* * *

I had been in Mitchell for about six months when suddenly and out of the blue the authorities approached me and asked if I would take on the duties of county coroner. This was considered at the time to be something of a 'plum job' carrying as it did some status and authority and indeed not a little excitement. It didn't take me long to accept the offer with enthusiasm and they gave me a book to read and some preliminary instructions on how to conduct a coroner's court and when to hold inquests and so on. The only downside as I saw it at the time was that I was required to swear an oath of allegiance to the queen of England as part of the initiation process to becoming a coroner to Perth County. This kind of oath-taking stuck in the craw somewhat but sure who would ever know and what the hell, I didn't mean one word of it and I did want to become a coroner.

I was busy enough at it too. What with seeing sixty to seventy patients in the afternoons in the office, visiting patients in hospital and assisting at surgery in the mornings, making house calls and being on call seven days a week, now on top of all that I was on call to the police at any moment, day or night, to visit the scene of a fatal accident, shooting, stabbing, murder or suicide. And suicides there were a plenty. In rural Ontario during the long cold winters farmers developed what was then referred to as 'cabin fever', a usually mildly depressive illness that we now call seasonal affective disorder or SAD syndrome. And they killed themselves, usually out in their barns either by hanging or shooting themselves. They typically shot themselves by placing the muzzle of a twelve-bore shotgun into their mouths and discharging the gun by using a length of binding-twine tied to their big toe and the trigger. When you were at a scene like this you would see brain tissue and fragments of skull embedded into the barn roof twenty feet above the unfortunate victim. These poor men must have led lives of quiet desperation. It was all so sad really. What is in the mind of a man who does this to himself?

And then there was the time that all the hot water ran out in an apartment block in Stratford. When the janitor went to investigate the cause of this he made a grim discovery in one of the basement flats. A young man lay face down in a full bath of water with the hot tap still running, now cold of course. He had been there for five days, a rope of 'soap on a rope' was wrapped around his neck, the soap itself long dissolved and gone. I ordered a post mortem because the whole thing looked so odd. This revealed a fractured skull with subsequent brain haemorrhage and damage. What appeared to have happened was that the young man, a known alcoholic, had slipped backwards and struck the back of his head off the taps and that was his undoing. I will never forget the smell in that bathroom.

There were road traffic accidents too, of course. These in the main were brutal, careless and horrendous carnages that will stay with me for all time. The worst of these, and they were all bad, actually happened in the village of Mitchell one Saturday evening. Drag-racing was all the rage at the time. To drag-race, two very powerful or souped-up cars line up at a given line and rev their engines up to maximum revolutions per second. On a given signal the drivers then let the clutch in and the cars take off like a rocket down a straight line. Whoever crosses the line first, 500 yards down the road, is the winner. Drag-racing is strictly for mindless morons. On a properly laid out circuit it is not too dangerous. But when a few young men attempt a bit of drag-racing down the main street of a village on a busy Saturday afternoon then you might expect some trouble. When the same young men are all fired up on booze and drugs then trouble is inevitable.

They used the traffic lights at the top of the street as a signal to start the drag-race. Things were going well enough until one of the cars lost control, mounted the pavement and ploughed into the innocent Saturday evening shoppers. Five people were killed instantly including the driver and his back-seat passenger, a young fellow called Beatles Bailey who I knew as a patient of mine with a drug problem. The three dead on the street included a young woman and her boyfriend. Her entire leg and buttock had been ripped clean away from her body by the impact and when I arrived on the scene seconds after the accident I could only look helplessly on as she rapidly exsanguinated from this massive wound and died in my arms. Her heart and brain were looking for blood but there was none. It was all out on the pavement in front of me and I could not put it back nor staunch its flow.

Afterwards I ordered an inquest into this wanton waste of young human life and the jury recommended a greater police presence to deter illegal drag-racing and greater fines and punishments for those caught so breaking the law. I have no idea if these recommendations were ever implemented. Coroner's courts then, as now, had minimal influence on society and human behaviour. A coroner's mission statement in Canada at that time was 'we speak for the dead to protect the living'. And while I understood that fully and indeed felt honoured to have been entrusted with such an onerous task, I remain sceptical as to how well this system works. Perhaps the best that can be said is that at least we tried.

* * *

Joni Mitchell's singing and writing and particularly her first album called *Blue* were hugely influential for both Ann and myself at this time. We played that record night and day until we had it worn almost smooth. The marriage at this juncture seemed to be going quite well. Of course we had the common bond of both of us being Irish emigrants and both agreeing that we would, sooner rather than later, return to our native shores. There was peace and love and very few fights.

Family and work commitments meant that sports and hobbies during my time in Canada had to be at a minimum. I was very lucky in that just down the road from us in Mitchell there was a skeet field where, under the guidance of my friend, Louis Morello, I learned how to shoot properly and only then understood how it was that I missed all those pheasants when shooting with Joe Ward a few years earlier. Skeet is a formal clay-pigeon layout where the targets are fired from two separate traps in opposite directions. The traps are housed in a 'high house' and a 'low house'. Skeet is shot in squads of five guns, each individual shooting in turn and all moving from station one under the 'high house' through six more stands set in a semi-circle until the eighth stand is reached set between the two houses. At some stands you are required to shoot only singles – left to right and right to left. At other stands you are required to shoot doubles when both traps are released together. A round of skeet comprises twenty-five shots per gun. The gun must be held off the shoulder until the target appears which is anytime up to three seconds after you shout, 'pull'. The whole thing is hugely demanding and requires your full concentration. It is also very sociable and good fun.

The only other way we had of shooting in Canada was at live pigeons driven out of barns. Pigeons tended to winter in farmers' barns where they ate scraps of grain and animal feed and crapped onto the farm machinery from their perches high up in the rafters. As such they were an awful nuisance to the farmers who were only too delighted to give us the opportunity to shoot at them. The far-mer would go into his barn and beat around it with a big stick driv-ing the pigeons out through a small aperture under the roof. You never knew if or when one might break for it and a lot more pigeons were missed than hit. But it was an amusing way of shooting.

We were not in Mitchell for too long before making some good friends, again as always, through our music and songs. Joan Gaffney played piano and did a perfect take on Gracie Field's 'The Biggest Aspidistra in the World' while her daughter, Dianne, played guitar and did Gordon Lightfoot stuff. Ann and I would sing a sea shanty together called 'Sally Brown', a great rollicking song with close harmony on the 'rolling go' bit:

> I shipped on board of a Liverpool liner
> Away hay and a rolling go
> We will roll all night and we'll roll till the day
> I am going to spend my money along with Sally Brown.

Ann might sing a Napoleon song that went:

> Bonaparte he commanded his troops for to stand
> And he planted his cannon all over the land
> He planted his cannon the whole victory for to gain
> And he killed my loyal horseman returning from Spain.

In our company often at these sessions would be John and Nancy Ferguson, John and Liz Moore, the Rubies, the Kellehers and maybe the Taylors from Belfast who were just discovering that there was such a thing as Irish music. We drank mostly Canadian beer in those days. I never could drink rye whiskey and Canadian wine, made from a grape called 'concord' was, in my opinion, utterly undrinkable.

One day a package arrived in the post that quite transformed our time in Canada. Remember at this stage we were starved of decent Irish music or singing. We missed our Hamilton Irish friends and while the Gaffneys were always generous to a fault their music was not quite what we needed. I had just purchased a state of the art quadrasonic Pioneer sound system. The package contained a copy of the just released *Prosperous* album recorded in the basement of this house and with a picture of the house on the front of the sleeve and my name mentioned twice on the back as having given Christy Moore two of the songs. When we put that record on to this sound system and turned up the volume we were quite simply blown away.

When Liam Óg O'Flynn, playing the uilleann pipes, broke into 'Tabhair dom do Lámh' or 'Give me your Hand' after Christy's first song 'The Raggle Taggle Gypsy', I wept for joy. That record was played morning, noon and night. I know every twist and turn of it and played along with it on the whistle where keys agreed.

* * *

News from the home front was not great. My parents, by then both well into their seventies, were involved in a horrible car crash while on their way back from Easter services in Maynooth College. A truck drove right out in front of them at a crossroads. My mother was taken to hospital where there was a failure to spot a fractured cervical vertebra on x-ray. This did not help her recovery one little bit. My father, while naturally very shaken, escaped otherwise un-injured. But this was serious news to have to bear and we were 3,000 miles from home. Given my work commitments as coroner and the difficulty of getting anyone to cover my large practice, getting away at short notice was not easy. But, one's first duties are to oneself and to one's family. Work and patient's welfare should at all times be secondary and doctors, including this one, often forget that.

Back in Ireland I find both my parents in the rehabilitation hospital in Dun Laoghaire. My mother is in a revolving bed on traction to help avoid spinal cord injury arising from her fractured neck. My father is sitting on the edge of his bed upset but very glad to see me. He smokes his Sweet Afton through a black cigarette holder. In time they would both recover but incompletely. At a certain age people never really recover from this kind of assault on their frail bodies. Returning to Canada at this time was very difficult but it had to be done.

Joy was on the way. On 17 March 1972 our long awaited daughter arrived delivered by a lady GP in Stratford General Hospital. St Patrick's Day and there we were with a baby daughter in a foreign land. We christened her Caoilfhionn, meaning the fair-haired one and there was much to celebrate. Both our children were, and of course remain, Canadian and Irish citizens, something that gives them more options should they choose to use them later in life.

* * *

If I have at times seemed to be somewhat critical of Mitchell and its good God-fearing citizens then perhaps I need to make amends. After all here I was, a blow-in and a bit of an impostor, and yet at least seventy per cent of the population of the town and the farmers and their families for a radius of ten miles or more supported my practice and were good and loyal patients of mine. It wasn't as though they had no choice. There were plenty of doctors ten miles away in Stratford and a few more over in Seaforth. Nor was it that I was a brilliant doctor with a lovely bedside manner and oozing with charm. Charm and bedside manner were never part of my armoury against disease and illness. I was practical and matter-of-fact and I think a reasonably good diagnostician. But charming? I hardly think so. No, these good and honest people supported my practice and me because for two and a half years of the four and a half that I spent there I was the only doctor in town and for that reason and that reason alone I think I had solid support and was made to feel that I was needed and that I belonged. And for that I owe the people of Mitchell, Ontario my eternal gratitude.

I did of course try to get help. I was running a single-handed general practice that should have been a two-doctor practice. I was on call all the time. I strongly believed in the concept of group practice and through the advertisement columns of the medical journals and magazines was all the time on the lookout for another doctor to join me. And besides all of that I knew that I was not going to stay there forever and eventually would need someone to take over. But good doctors were very scarce at that particular time and the few that were around wanted to live in the 'smart' places like London, Ontario or Stratford. Mitchell was seen as something of a backwater, which it was of course, but backwaters too can have their own charm. But try telling that to a young GP just out of training.

Eventually, having been there on my own for two and a half years a second doctor did arrive and set himself up in an office on the main street of Mitchell. Dr Bob Lorimer was a surly Scotsman with an attitude problem against Ireland and the Irish that I never quite understood. I thought everyone loved the Irish but Dr Lorimer was going to dissuade me from such arrogance. But, far more serious than that, Bob had an issue with the demon drink, which was eventually to bring about his early demise. He died from ruptured oesophageal varicoceles, a complication of alcohol-induced liver cirrhosis. He was only in his mid-forties. Because I drink myself and always have done perhaps I am not the best at spotting it when a colleague has a real drinking problem. I did not actually realise at the time how serious Bob's problem was. It is only now when I think back and picture him in my mind's eye and see him sitting on his sundeck at lunchtime with a very large Scotch whiskey in one hand and a can of beer in the other that I wonder just how blind can I have been.

Anyway, drinking problem or no drinking problem, Dr Lorimer and I set up a rota system together which meant that at long last I could have every second night and every second weekend off duty and quite suddenly my quality of life and that of my very young family improved immeasurably. This happy situation was to last for the next two years until we folded our tent and returned to Ireland for good.

Word was out that they had no doctor in Clane, county Kildare. Dr Michael Walsh, who I had known quite well and whose practice I had designs on, had died suddenly. He was only in his early seventies and was, I always believed, killed by overwork. He was of the old dispensary doctor school of practice. These doctors always worked alone and died young. But this event took us somewhat by surprise and of course we couldn't just uproot and come home at a minute's notice to take 'advantage' of the vacancy left by Dr Walsh's death. It was however the catalyst that set events in motion and told us that the time had come for us to start our process of repatriation back to Ireland. We put our new house on the market and sold it within a few weeks with a closing date set for six months hence. I put an advertisement in the medical journals seeking a doctor to replace me. Now the die was truly cast and there was no going back. Were we making the right decision?

Our friends the Gaffneys, the Moores, the Fergusons and the Rubies all thought that we were mad and in fact were genuinely exasperated with us. My nurse, Anne Rowland, and secretary, Ina Moses, were, I am sorry to say, quite hurt also by our decision to go home. My colleague Bob Lorimer thought we were daft. And I can see their point now perhaps better than then. There I was with a large thriving and solid medical practice, which was earning me a very considerable income. I was county coroner and had only just turned thirty years of age. I had a lovely house, a wife and two healthy young children. I had my hospital practice and special skill in vasectomy. The world was at our feet. And yet we were going to deliberately and wilfully turn our backs on all of that and simply walk away from it and return to Ireland to nothing. Yes, put that way I can of course see that our friends had a good point.

But this is the point that really can't be explained to others because it is all about feelings, soul and emotions: when we thought about putting down roots and staying on in Canada for the rest of our lives we thought about our Irish colleagues who had made just that decision. We saw that look in their eyes and, in spite of their protesting otherwise, we felt their sadness and loss and we were absolutely determined not to join them, however good they thought their lives to be. But how can you explain that to others?

CHAPTER 8
Back Home Again

On 3 January 1974, a cold, sleety, blustery day, we parked the car outside the garda station in Naas while going into the Manor Inn for a bite to eat. My sister pointed out a pink rose that was more or less still in bloom and asked if I was impressed with the way things still grow during the winter in Ireland. 'I bet you would never see the likes of that in Canada,' she said proudly. But to be quite honest with you I was tired and jetlagged and confused and at that precise time could not have cared less what pink rose grew when or where. Selling our house in Canada and packing all our worldly goods into a car-sized crate and handing my practice over to Dr Bill Payne, saying goodbye to all our good friends in Mitchell and wondering all the while if we were doing the right thing; all of this draining activity had taken its emotional toll on both of us so discussions about extended growing seasons seemed hugely irrelevant.

Our first shock on returning to Ireland after five and a half years in exile was the discovery that there were so few houses available for sale. While in Canada I had invested in a number of houses over the years in Newbridge and elsewhere but we needed to set up in or near Clane, county Kildare where I hoped to establish my medical practice and there quite simply were no houses on the market. Before leaving Canada we had arranged with our old friends Billy and Bridie Travers that we would stay in their guesthouse, Curry Hills House, just outside Prosperous until we found a suitable house to buy. But we thought that would only be a matter of a few weeks at the most. In fact we stayed in Curry Hills for eight full weeks until we bought a semi-detached house in a housing estate outside Clane called Loughbollard. This was not really what we wanted but we had no choice and it would have to make do for the moment.

Our next big annoyance was that our car-sized crate that Luis Marello had made for us and containing all our worldly possessions was being held up in Montreal as a result of some industrial dispute or other. Nobody could tell us exactly where our crate was, much less throw any light on the question as to when, if ever, it might reach us. It contained our beds and furniture and sound equipment and records and two shotguns. But, much more importantly, it contained all my surgical and medical equipment including an examining table, weighing scales, sphygmomanometers and doctor's bag, all of which I now urgently needed in order to start a new general practice.

My first surgery was located in the basement of the parish priest's house on the main street in Clane which Fr Hughes very kindly let me have, rent-free, until something else turned up. By this time, almost a year after his death, Dr Walsh's old practice had all but dissipated so things were very slow indeed. And on top of that I had another problem. In Ireland, then as now, about a third of the population were given a medical card allowing them free access to a doctor of their choice. But not all doctors were allowed access to this so-called free choice of doctor scheme. You had to be in practice in an area for five years before you could be considered for inclusion in the scheme and, in the meantime, you were expected to eke out a living on whatever private practice you could find. Pickings were thin on the ground.

So here I was now twiddling my thumbs down in the basement of Fr Hughes' old house and a little later on twiddling my thumbs up in the old dispensary house where the late Dr Walsh once lived. A few months ago I was seeing sixty patients a day. I had two secretaries and a nurse. I had admitting rights to a good local hospital and I was county coroner and now this desolation and abandonment. But of course there was no one to blame, no one to complain to. All of this I had knowingly, willingly and voluntarily brought down upon myself. This was nonetheless a deeply depressing period of my life with an empty waiting-room and all self-confidence dwindling. Why did nobody want my services? Things could only get better and they did.

In or around April of this, my first year home from Canada, news broke that the Irish Family Planning Association was about to offer a vasectomy service for Irish men. You would have to have lived through those years to know just how ground-breaking and radical this development was. Ireland then, and indeed for several years more, was in the iron grip of the Catholic Church which of course forbade all artificial means of contraception including the birth control pill. It is not that we were all Holy Joes or anything like that. It was just that people were almost brainwashed into believing that sexual activity, even within marriage, had always to leave open the possibility for procreation otherwise it was quite simply evil or at least sinful. This is what was being drummed into them practically every Sunday from the altar and it took considerable courage to stand up and to question this obsessive dogma that was being rammed down people's throats by a supposedly celibate clergy.

Even as late as the mid-1970s there was this unwritten presumption that if certain practices were forbidden by the Church then all of us, Catholic, Protestant and Atheist alike, were supposed to knuckle under and toe the line. There was a strict network in place to ensure that the status quo was upheld and those who would dare raise objections did so at their peril. Secretive male-dominated clubs and societies like the Knights of Columbanus, Opus Dei and Catholic League of Decency infiltrated the powerhouses of Irish politics, Irish medicine, Irish law and Irish education. Thus if you went to Dr X enquiring if he might prescribe the contraceptive pill you most likely were going to be refused on some quasi-medical pretence, though the real reason was that Dr X was a member of the Legion of Mary.

Or your marriage was in trouble or you were being abused by a drunken loutish husband and you discussed this with solicitor Y. The proper advice should be to move out of the house and sue the abusing husband. But solicitor Y might advise you to hang in there because he was a member of the Knights of Columbanus and did not approve of divorce or separation.

People who held and who still hold these views of course have every right to do so and I have always respected that right. But holding those views, even if the majority shares them, does not give anyone the right to scramble up on high moral ground and impose these rules on the rest of us in what we like to think of as a secular society.

Often in those days I would be asked by a woman with say, six children, if I thought it would be all right if she took the pill. She wouldn't be asking me if I thought it would be all right from a medical viewpoint. No, she wanted to know if I thought it would be morally all right for her to use contraceptives. Or, in other words, doctors were sometimes looked upon as kind of surrogate priests, a role that I for one thought quite absurd. Frequently when people were leaving the surgery they would mistakenly say, 'Thank you very much, Father' before correcting themselves. But if there was all this hysteria about the birth control pill you can just imagine what a brouhaha there was going to be about sterilisation or vasectomy.

The first session of four vasectomies in Ireland was conducted at the Irish Family Planning Association's premises on Mountjoy Square in Dublin during the summer of 1974. The operator was a lady ophthalmic surgeon who had been flown into Ireland especially for the occasion. I was there too because as soon as I heard that the IFPA was setting up this service I had phoned them up to say that I had experience in about one hundred vasectomies from Canada and wanted to know if I could be of any service to them. In response to this they asked that I join with the ophthalmic surgeon and do the last operation on the list in order to demonstrate that I knew what I was talking about and that I could in fact do a vasectomy. All of that I thought was fair enough. After all I could have been anyone just chancing my arm as far as they were concerned and as always patient safety was number one. I carried out the last vasectomy on the list without any problems and the ophthalmic surgeon declared me a safe pair of hands and the rest is, as they say, history.

Being taken on at that particular time by the IFPA to do the three or four vasectomies that they then had per week was extremely fortuitous from my point of view. The tiny private practice that I had built up by that stage was hardly sufficient to put bread on the table and this additional work was exactly what I needed right now. This was all pure luck and was a matter of just being in the right place at the right time. Had I returned from Canada three months later someone else would have got the job and I would have missed this opportunity altogether. It soon got around to my colleagues in general practice that I was doing vasectomies for the IFPA and they then started to refer the odd patient to me also. So between my weekly sessions at Synge Street family planning clinic and a trickle of private vasectomies referred to me by my colleagues there was less pressure on me now to build up a general practice in a hurry. This could be allowed to grow organically as it were, which is really the only way that these things happen anyway.

Not indeed that all my hospital colleagues were that enamoured with the idea of a mere GP doing minor surgery outside of the hospital setting. They hated to see happening what they perceived as a loss of control. But the fact of the matter was that the consultant urologists of the day did not know how to do a vasectomy and even if they did were not at liberty to carry them out in their Catholic-controlled institutions.

When I had carried out my first 631 vasectomies at Synge Street, where Nurse Marie Lee was my assistant, Dr Harry Counihan approached me one day to know if I might like to publish a paper on the subject of vasectomy in its Irish context. Harry was then the editor of the *Irish Medical Journal*. The paper was to describe how a vasectomy was done, the age profile of those having it done, the average number of children they had and describe any complications encountered with these first 631 cases. I thought that this was a splendid idea and agreed immediately to gather my statistics and start writing this paper. Little did I know what was coming next.

In due course my paper was ready for publication. As is the way with these things, it was all very formally laid out with tables and figures and graphs and references. There are strict rules and protocols pertaining to the way one approaches the writing of what we call a 'peer-review' medical paper. The average age of men presenting for vasectomy at that time was 34.9 years, the average number of children that they had was 3.8 children. Were we to repeat this study today we would find that both of those figures had fallen quite considerably. Today the average family size for a man presenting for vasectomy would be in the region of 2.4 children while they also tend to be younger with an average age of about 32 years.

I mentioned the formal way that this paper had to be laid out only because this factor gave me some comfort, false comfort as it turned out, that my work would remain buried in academia, never to see the light of day through the popular press. That was the way I needed it to be. Both my parents were alive at the time and I did not want to upset them by their learning of my wanton anti-Catholic ways. To use the modern parlance, I was not yet ready to 'come out' on the subject of vasectomy. But, if I thought that the popular media were not going to pick up on my article in the *Irish Medical Journal*, then the *Sunday World* had a surprise for me. The very next Sunday after my piece was published in the *Irish Medical Journal*, the *Sunday World* seized upon it in the worst way possible. Right on the front page and in true tabloid fashion the headline roared out to my parents coming out from mass:

IRISH DOCTOR STERILISES 631 MEN IN DUBLIN CLINIC.

So that was it. The cat was out of the bag. My father took it very badly indeed. That day he phoned Fr Hughes, the parish priest of Clane, who was now a neighbour of ours. We had just moved across the street from him into a Victorian house called St Ann's. My father asked that the priest go over to my house and have a word with me. Someone raised the possibility of excommunication as a way of dealing with me. The priest duly called over, having phoned me in advance. To be fair about it he was all sweetness and light. He did not want to be there in the first place and only came over because he had promised my irate father that he would. We opened a bottle of Jameson and got stuck into that. But it was a no win situation and both of us knew it. I had no intention of discontinuing vasectomies since I have always felt that this was a private matter and it was up to an individual's conscience. I was in no mood for religious dictates and that was that. We parted that evening good friends, agreeing to differ and, in the fullness of time, everybody settled down, including my father.

Although all of this was something that I would have much preferred had never happened it is, as we all know, an ill wind that does not blow some good. The *Sunday World* at that time had a huge circulation and this was banner headlines front-page coverage. Were we to pay for this kind of advertising you would be looking at tens of thousands of euro at today's rates. If there were any men in Ireland who did not know that vasectomy was now available here before the *Sunday World* quoted my article then there were very few of them left afterwards. Business started to rise steadily. Synge Street family planning clinic was still the only centre in Ireland offering vasectomy so they came from far and wide, from Kerry to Donegal, Wexford to Louth. In time more centres would open up but for the first three or four years we had the entire country to ourselves.

This was not my only brush with the clergy. Another parish priest from a neighbouring parish phoned me up wanting to know if he could come and see me in my own house. When I got this phone call I thought to myself, this is great, I'll have a parish priest on my list of patients and that will do no end of good in lifting my practice profile as it were. But the priest had different plans for me.

When he arrived Fr Mulvihill greeted me cordially and walked straight into the drawing-room. And no thank you he didn't want tea or coffee and as for the other stuff he never touched it. Things were off to an ominous start. Once in the large room the priest starts going around to the pictures hanging on the wall and, with his hands held behind his back, peers at each one trying to make out the artist's signature and then he makes some inane comment or other as to his opinion on the artistic merits of the picture in question. He throws out the odd question like 'Are any of these rumours that I have been hearing about you true?' Since I'm not quite sure to which rumours he was referring, I kick for touch and say 'of course not'.

'Oh that's good,' says the priest.

Three pictures later and another artist identified and commented upon the priest holds out his left little finger to me and inquires if he were to ask me to chop it off would I oblige. This I understood to be an oblique reference to mutilation, a pejorative sometimes heaped on vasectomy by those opposed to the operation for whatever reason. But at this stage I had had just about enough of this meddling cleric offering me his version of gratuitous moral guidance. As politely as I could, though at this stage I was getting quite annoyed, I informed the man of the cloth that if ever I felt the need for his counselling on medical ethics that he would be the very first to know and that in the meantime I would be most obliged if he would leave my house. He did, saying that he was most relieved to hear that none of those rumours he had been hearing about me had a shred of truth to them and that he felt that that was the case all along. The incident was not without its funny side.

But it was also extremely galling. That a priest should have the audacity and bare-face impudence to come into someone's house and to in effect deliver to the occupants a lecture on his own home-grown version of morality was quite simply outrageous. Suppose the boot was on the other foot for a moment. Suppose that I phoned up this parish priest and told him that I needed to have a word with him and would it be all right if I went into his house and spoke to him. Then suppose on arrival I started to peer at his pictures and tell him that in my view he was grossly overweight, clearly was eating all the wrong foods and not taking nearly enough exercise and if he didn't mend his ways that soon he was in for an early and painfully slow death. How long do you think it would take the priest to show me the door and rightly so?

But it wasn't all doom and gloom by any means. Up in Synge Street family planning clinic where I was doing all those vasectomies and was for three years the only doctor in Ireland so engaged, we also had the occasional laugh as well. We had this background music playing from one of those old eight-track tape players. They are defunct now but at this time in the early 1980s they were considered state of the art technology. This classical music was supposed to relax the clients who might be understandably apprehensive about what they were soon to undergo. As such though I never gave any thought as to the content of this piped music and in time, like traffic noise or the sound of a rookery, never heard it at all.

One day we had this man on the table and we were well into the second half of his vasectomy and everything was going grand. Then suddenly out of the blue the man says: 'Jesus I don't believe it!'

'You don't believe what?' Marie my nurse wanted to know.

'I don't believe the music you're playing in the background there.' We all stop and listen. I'm not sure because classical music at the time was not my forte. But the patient on the table was in no doubt whatsoever: 'That's the "Nut Cracker Suite",' he informed us with justifiable outrage. From that moment onwards Tchaikovsky was taken off the menu of our in-house entertainment package.

Another time we had a clinical photographer in taking a series of photographs of a vasectomy being performed. I had been asked to give a lecture on the subject of vasectomy and needed to augment this talk with a series of slides each showing the various stages of the procedure – the local anaesthetic, the incision, the grasping of the vas with this special forceps and so on like that. Each photograph was a close-up on the scrotum only with the rest of the patient being off camera.

The man having the vasectomy and at the same time having a series of photographs being taken of the operation was very much amused by the whole thing and was wearing a broad grin on his face throughout the entire proceedings. Marie was gifted with a fine Dublin sense of humour. When she saw him grinning away at the camera she said to him: 'You do not have to smile for these photographs you know.'

* * *

My parents' health continued to be of concern. My father's rheuma-toid arthritis had perhaps passed its worst but he had another prob-lem equally incurable then as it is today. Macular degeneration is an insidious blinding disease that affects the back of the eye or retina. If you think of the eye as a small camera then the retina is the film or that part of the eye that captures the image and relays it via the optic nerve to the brain. The retina is a delicate structure fed by tiny little blood vessels. If these vessels are in any way compromised then damage is inevitable. Macular degeneration runs in my family. My father, and now two cousins, had been affected. In order to re-duce my chances of getting it I take a daily dose of Zinc along with a good multivitamin capsule. Studies have shown that this nutri-tional approach should reduce my chances of developing macular degeneration by at least thirty per cent

My mother's health if anything was even worse. For a woman who never drank or smoked and who did all the 'right things' all her life she was very unlucky to have had a small stroke when in her sixties and then to develop Parkinson's-like symptoms later on.

Up in the big house my brother and sister-in-law are getting restless and unsettled. The house is too big for them and whatever interest Davoc ever had in farming he is rapidly losing it. Clare beck-ons them. Clare is the ancestral birthplace of the Rynnes. Our people all come from Cluana and Clunnaha outside of Ennistymon. Clare moreover is probably the best county in Ireland for traditional Irish music, something Anne and Davoc are very interested in. There are perhaps more romantic than practical overtones to this notion of taking up roots and settling in Spanish Point but that is what they are intent on doing. Soon the big house will be empty but not for long.

Over in Robertstown the canal festivals are in full swing and that hurricane of a man Fr P. J. Murphy drives that sleepy little vil-lage into action making the once near derelict Grand Canal Hotel a major tourist attraction. Fr Murphy was a classic example of just what can be achieved given enough enthusiasm, drive and energy. When he was killed in a car crash a few years later the whole

Robertstown project fell on its face never to recover. But we had some great years there. Along with Ned Farrell acting as host, playing the bodhrán and telling funny stories and Gerry O'Mahony on box and Frank Burke on fiddle, I was asked to join as singer and occasional whistle player. We dressed up in sort of Georgian costumes with knee breeches and white stockings and wigs that didn't really fit us. At half time we would go into Mulannies next door to slake our thirst. It really was more of the same and shades of the Abbey Tavern fifteen years earlier – drinking, playing and earning a few bob for doing what we all loved.

By now Downings House was empty and idle and sad. If it was left that way for long it would start to moulder and reach a point of no return. It needed major work done to it while it was still relatively dry inside. I negotiated with my sister to purchase the house and an adjoining eleven acres of woodlands and pasture. All the windows needed replacing, it needed to be re-plastered all around, rewired and plumbed, a central heating system installed and a new roof fitted. All of this work was commenced in June 1979 and finished at the end of November that same year. Just at that time it was easy to find good craftsmen because there was a lull in the building industry. That's why I was able to get all the work done so quickly. By Christmas we had sold St Ann's on Clane's main street and had moved back into the house that I was born in. All of this, like most things in life, happened not by design but by happenstance.

I believe Ann viewed this move to the large house as something of a mixed blessing. For me it was different of course. It was where I was born and where I grew up. But for Ann there were no such emotional attachments to alleviate the impracticality of the whole thing. She once referred to the house as a 'glorified wind tunnel', which was probably quite accurate and certainly quite witty. But the house and the unsatisfactory land division that I negotiated with my sister was undoubtedly another nail in the coffin of an already shaky marriage.

A year after moving into Downings we applied to the Eastern Health Board to adopt a child. The screening process for potential adoptive parents was, as it remains today, long, gruelling and personally invasive. It was also incompetent because it failed to unearth the cracks that must have been already appearing in our marriage. In due course a three-year-old boy called Adam was identified as a probable candidate. Adam was of mixed parentage – his father Nigerian, his mother Irish. We took him in and loved him as one of our own. But when he reached maturity he flew the coop and today sadly we have almost no contact with him at all. But sometimes adoption can be like that. Sometimes, no matter how hard you try, adopted children are never quite yours and perhaps this is understandable at a certain level. Adopting is not always the same as natural parenting; at least it wasn't to be for Ann and I. That is not to say that the whole experience was not worthwhile and hugely rewarding in itself. A sad ending but perhaps adoptive parents should not always assume a long-term relationship.

* * *

Robert Brook built the village of Prosperous in 1780. Brook made his money by collecting rents in India – nice work if you can get it. He invested almost a million pounds of his own money in setting up a cotton industry and building the village of Prosperous for its workers. The houses were all to be of brick and slate and each to have enough land to graze a cow. Many of these houses survive today such that, in the old part of the village, you can still easily appreciate the broad Georgian streetscape with its two small squares.

The glory days for Prosperous were short lived. In spite of receiving two grants from Grattan's parliament amounting to almost two million pounds, this massive project never really got off the ground. Brook blamed drunkenness among the workers but the truth in fact may have lain closer to home. For a start the location was wrong and the concept too grandiose. Very little product was ever produced from the cotton mills and the whole venture folded within a few years. The successful battle of Prosperous in 1798 nearly finished the place off for good. Lewis, commenting in 1837, describes Prosperous as 'little more than a pile of ruins situated in a low marshy spot, surrounded by bogs and without water of importance nor reasonable hope for its revival'. I am glad to say Lewis got it all wrong. Today Prosperous is a vibrant little community with new people moving in all the time. In 1980 I was chairman of the bicentenary committee when, thanks to the creativity of Nan Clark, we had a week of activities ending with the unveiling of a monument beside Healy's post-office. Here we placed a plaque on the wall commemorating Robert Brook.

Soon after these celebrations my father had to have a leg amputated due to gangrene that in turn was brought on by narrowing of the artery supplying blood to his leg. A life-long habit of over twenty cigarettes a day had eventually caught up with him in his seventy-ninth year. I went to visit him in the Richmond Hospital the day after the amputation and, while he may have lost a leg, he clearly had not lost his sense of humour. 'I suppose they'd say that this operation was a great success,' he said to me with an impish grin on his face. He died the next day but I think that he had suffered enough and that it was time to go.

Being the doctor in the family certain tasks seemed to fall on me 'naturally' and it was left to me to impart the bad news to my mother who was, by then, confined to a nursing home. When she saw the look on my face as I came into her room she instinctively knew and anticipated my sad message. This made my task a little easier and she took the news with great calm and poise. She died herself six months later. She too had had enough.

CHAPTER 9

A Storm in a Condom

Contraceptives were totally outlawed in Ireland under section 17 of the Criminal Law Amendment Act 1935. This act makes it quite clear that it is 'unlawful to sell, or expose, offer, advertise or keep for sale or to import or attempt to import into Saorstat Éireann any contraceptive'. Since neither the birth control pill nor the intra-uterine contraceptive device (IUCD) had yet been invented the term 'contraceptive' in section 17 is taken to mean condoms exclusively. How such a clearly sectarian statute could find its way into the legislature of a so-called republic is very difficult to understand. Other European countries that once had similar legislation had long since scrapped it. Fortunately for me vasectomy had not been invented in 1935. Otherwise I have little doubt but that it too would have been squeezed in under the terms of this act.

It may be tempting to suspect that the Catholic hierarchy had a lean on the government to keep this legislation in the statute books. But in fact they did not need to overly interfere because they had a laity who were more than capable of doing the infiltrating for them. Deeply conservative groups like the Legion of Mary, the Catholic League of Decency, the Irish Family League and most particularly the all-male and secretive Knights of Columbanus were well represented on government benches and within the medical and legal professions. These were the self-appointed custodians of the common morality and the occupiers of the high moral ground.

Protestantism is a minority religion in the Republic of Ireland. Protestants do not share with Catholics a moral veto on contraception or birth control. So why did Irish Protestants not protest against this blatantly sectarian piece of legislation? I wish I knew.

I suppose one must try to understand the concerns of people at the time even if one did not always share them. Reading the letter columns of our national newspapers around 1972 and 1973, it seems many people expressed their opposition to contraceptives in terms of the perceived disastrous consequences of 'introducing that kind of filth' into Ireland. To further justify these fears they would point to other countries, usually to the UK and say: 'look at what happened over there'. The principles that one was being asked to take on board were: (a) that Irish sexual morality was superior to elsewhere in the world and (b) one of the reasons why that was so was because there were no contraceptives. The fact that there was not a shred of evidence to support either proposition did not seem to matter.

It was left to a Catholic mother of four, Mrs Mary McGee, then aged only twenty-seven, to take a High Court and later a Supreme Court action against the government in 1973. Mary's contraceptives had been seized in the post by customs. She had a history of toxaemia of pregnancy (a potentially fatal complication that tends to get worse with each ensuing pregnancy) and was advised not to have any more children. She claimed before the Supreme Court that by seizing her contraceptives the state was denying her her constitutional right to privacy including marital privacy. A very brave young woman, Mary McGee won her case and this precedent put an enormous dent in the efficacy of the 1935 act to keep contraceptives out of Holy Ireland.

Following this ruling the clause dealing with 'import or attempt to import' was no longer sustainable. Anticipating this outcome Senator Mary Robinson attempted to introduce a Private Members bill to legislate for the new post-McGee situation but the government refused to even discuss it. It seemed that they were happier to have a deeply flawed prohibition on contraception than to actually face up to introducing laws that squared with the Irish Supreme Court ruling.

The exact same scenario repeated itself many years later when the Supreme Court ruled on a constitutional amendment to do with abortion. This ruling allows for abortion in Ireland where the mother's life is at serious risk but to date no matching legislation has been put in place and I very much doubt if it ever will be, at least not in my lifetime.

So there we were in the Irish Family Planning Association importing condoms to beat the band. The fractured Criminal Law Amendment Act 1935 still prohibited us from selling them so we gave them away for nothing instead and accepted a 'donation'. Strangely this donation always covered our costs with a decent profit thrown in for good measure. In those days it was all to do with language. The contraceptive pill likewise in theory was prohibited by the 1935 act but we got around this by calling it a 'cycle regulator' which was very handy.

And that's how things stood from 1973 until 1 November 1980 when the then minister for Health, Mr C. J. Haughey, introduced his inspired Health (Family Planning) Act 1979, the infamous 'Irish solution to an Irish problem' that made us the laughing stock of Europe if not indeed the whole world. In a nutshell this ludicrous piece of legislation made condoms a matter for a doctor's prescription and they could then only be dispensed by a community pharmacist. Note that under this arrangement, a person seeking contraceptives could not just go in and buy them from a GP or a pharmacist. No, a responsible adult, seeking to exercise his constitutional right to limit his family size, had to make two separate trips to two separate professionals and pay professional fees at each stop.

I felt from the beginning that this piece of legislation was grossly iniquitous, unworkable and a violation of human rights. As a doctor I felt a deep sense of disgust that my chosen profession had agreed to co-operate with this kind of hypocrisy. Also the political cowardliness and the craven way that the proposed legislation seemed to pander to a particular view of morality was, I found, deeply depressing. I strongly felt that if this were the best that Mr Haughey could come up with he would have been better off leaving the thing alone.

A doctor's prescription, or so I was always led to believe, was for serious medicines like antibiotics, addictive sedatives and analgesics like opiates and morphine and things that, in the public interest, need to be controlled. But condoms are not medicines or drugs, they are made from inert latex so what are they doing on a doctor's prescription? It was clear from the very beginning that this proposed new legislation was being foisted onto us in an awkward attempt to 'medicalise' our national neurosis about things sexual and to let the government off the hook. But we accepted it.

But it was even worse than that. The responsible adult seeking a package of condoms so as to prevent his wife from becoming pregnant could only get a prescription for them from the doctor for 'bona fide family planning purposes or for adequate medical reasons'. So here now was a brand new role for doctors to play. We were now being asked to make a judgement about our patient's morality when heretofore all that used to concern us was our patient's health. One implication of Mr Haughey's Health (Family Planning) Act was that if doctors suspected that their patients were going to use condoms for some purpose other than 'bona fide family planning' then that doctor was duty bound to refuse that patient a prescription. Doctors had to exercise great care in making this moral judgement about their patients because any laxity in this regard could result in the doctor facing a fine of £500 or six months imprisonment.

So why did the Irish medical profession accept this legislation which distorted the doctor–patient relationship and sought to exploit people who were just looking for condoms? Our collective opinion on this proposed new law was never sought. Mr Haughey discussed the proposal with the Irish Medical Association of the day and they agreed to accept it on our behalf. It was all to do with money. The Health (Family Planning) Act 1979 would bring increased business for general practitioners and therefore how could they object to it so why bother even asking them? But I believe that had this proposed legislation been put to a proper ballot of all doctors in Ireland, following proper debate, the vast majority of them would have rejected it.

As if to underline this notion that money would assuage us all I had a chance encounter with Mr Haughey after the press reception to launch his new Family Planning bill. Ann and I were at a reception given by the *Irish Medical Times* when in walked the minister. A small man, he walked with great economy of effort. He came into the room as if he was being pulled along on wheels for he took short but rapid steps, his arms held motionless by his side. Ann and I went right up to him and told him what we thought of his new bill. To this Mr Haughey replied that if I did not like it, then, as the bill stipulated, there was no obligation on me to participate, I could just opt out. This response was delivered with a backwards wave of his right hand as if he was trying to get rid of a housefly that had landed on the sugar bowl. It was a dismissive answer from an arrogant little man and it showed how the minister failed to grasp or perhaps did not want to grasp the serious flaws in his new legislation.

After this rather terse exchange Mr Haughey then addressed the assembled doctors. His opening words were: 'I will make money for you doctors yet'. It was difficult to decide which was the more painful, the tastelessness and insensitivity of a minister for Health who would make such a remark or the vulgarity and crassness of the assembled doctors who thought that this was funny. It hardly matters. I left that gathering feeling like a complete outsider, ashamed to be a doctor and very alone, sick to the pit of my stomach at the whole lot of them. It was then that I vowed to do whatever I could to bring this piece of legislation down and to expose it for the hypocrisy that it surely was.

The new laws surrounding the sale and distribution of condoms threw the Irish Family Planning Association into something of a backspin. As its newly-elected chairman I had to tread an impartial path. The sale of condoms, or should I say the giving away of condoms for nothing and the accepting of a 'donation', had been the organisation's main source of income and now all that was seriously threatened. There were two schools of thought as to what we should do. One was that we should simply ignore the law, carry on and see what would happen. This would have been my favoured approach because I saw the IFPA as a trail-blazing and pioneering organisation and had absolutely no respect for this new legislation. The association may have been pioneering at one time but by now, over a decade since its foundation, many of the people working in it were becoming institutionalised in their thinking and were fearful that if we broke the law we could be closed down and then they would all lose their jobs.

In the end it was these people who won out and the Irish Family Planning Association became fully compliant, or at least as compliant as possible, with the provisions of the Health (Family Planning) Act 1979. I had little choice but to accede to the majority view. A pharmacy division was established within the organisation and a full-time pharmacist was employed to oversee it. In this way the doctors could 'write' prescriptions for condoms and our pharmacist could 'dispense' them. In practice however prescriptions were written in bulk and the condoms were dispensed by whoever happened to be around at the time. But in theory at least we were compliant and it looked well and in any case there was never any attempt to enforce this law as the government did not need any embarrassing prosecutions.

This was so typically Irish but madly frustrating for all of that. We had an unworkable piece of legislation that shamelessly exploited people seeking to be responsible about family planning; everyone was breaking the law in all but spirit and nobody did anything to change it.

Outside of the IFPA it was difficult to know what we could do to challenge this wretched legislation. Dr Sheila Jones and I organised a petition with the signatures of some 260 doctors across Ireland saying that they were strongly opposed to this new law and that they would not cooperate. We drummed up as much publicity as we could and on 11 March 1982 delivered our letter to Dáil Éireann to Dr Michael Woods' secretary. Woods was minister for Health at this stage and Haughey, prime minister. It may not seem like much now but to get 260 doctors in Ireland to agree to anything was quite an achievement. But the thing got very little media attention and of course I am still waiting to hear back from Dr Woods.

As time went on it began to dawn on me that the only way to

bring embarrassing outside attention to this miserable legislation and thus have it changed was to go out and deliberately break the law. Since there was no effort being made to enforce it in the first place breaking it would have to be done in a very formal and documented way. The situation required some bottle. In July 1982 I asked a friend of mine, Robert Sheridan, to play a cameo role for me in this charade. He would come into my surgery at half past six in the evening and ask me for a package of ten condoms. I was then to sell him these directly and contrary to the provisions of Mr Haughey's Health (Family Planning) Act 1979. My 'excuse' for doing it this way was that the local pharmacy closed at 6 p.m. and I did not want my client to risk causing an unwanted pregnancy. I was to issue Mr Sheridan with a receipt for the money he paid me and this, along with a covering letter, would be sent off to the DPP for his consideration. This forced the government to act through its own DPP. Much as they may have wanted to do otherwise they simply could not ignore me.

We then sat back wondering what would happen next. After about two weeks the gardaí phoned me and asked if it would be all right if they 'raided' my surgery sometime as there had been a complaint made against me. I said that there would be no need for that, that they could come down here anytime they liked and that I would give them whatever they wanted. Such compliance among the criminal classes must be rare. A day or so later two burly gardaí arrived and I gave them a few packets of condoms and a receipt book showing that I had indeed been selling condoms directly to people contrary to the provisions of you know what. Then it was just a question of waiting another week or so for the summons to arrive.

* * *

During these years a group of four of us – James Egan, James O'Dwyer, Peter Cunningham and myself – used to take land for rough shooting down in Carlow, halfway between Rathvilly and Hackettstown. This land was for the most part poor for farming but ideal for snipe and released pheasants shooting. Two men used to look after things down there for us. We called them the 'Two Billys'. These men reared a few pheasants for us and came out with us, with their dogs, to keep the farmers sweet and, as best they could, to keep poachers away. The system worked very well for a good few years but the farmers were constantly improving their lands through drainage. This, while no doubt improving the land, left it unsuitable for snipe-shooting. As well as that it was becoming increasingly difficult to keep the farmers on our side and a time came when the thing became untenable.

But when it was working well we would go down to Carlow maybe four or five times during the shooting season, arriving at an appointed gateway at around 9.30 a.m. having stopped off for breakfast on the way down. We would then shoot until 12.30 or so, at which stage someone would deem it time for lunch which was, often as not, partaken of in a local hostelry called the Tobanstown Inn. In those days most country pubs did not serve any food at all so we would bring our own. By the time we'd get back to the Two Billys we would, as they say, be feeling very little pain.

After one such excellent lunch I remember we were taken onto a large field of sugar beet not yet harvested. This kind of a crop is great for holding pheasants particularly if it is a bit weedy. The pointer was sent out in front of the guns and the Two Billys followed behind. The pointer ranged right to left and left to right across the guns, her nose held close to the ground all the while trying to pick up a scent on this winter's day. Suddenly the dog stops dead in her tracks as if struck by lightning. She is petrified and statuesque. Her head is cocked slightly to one side, her front left paw is held off the ground, her tail is held out behind her as straight as a die. All the guns know that there is a cock pheasant somewhere about ten feet in front of the dog's nose and ready themselves accordingly. Dog and bird are going through their ancient ritualistic stand off.

Then the pointer begins to wag her tail in the horizontal plane, the tip moving two inches each way. This is a sure sign that the pheasant is about to move which is exactly what happens. The dog now breaks her set and moves slowly forward, crouched down. This is where you need a good steady dog. It is vital that the pointer keeps her distance behind the running pheasant otherwise he will break out of range of the guns and that is no good. The chase is on. The pointer moves on up the field in pursuit of the unseen bird. Peter Cunningham, who happens to be nearest to the action, takes off up the field after the running pheasant and crouched down pointer. This trio move forward from the rest of us by some 200 yards.

And then they all stop dead. The pheasant presumably has stopped running, the pointer goes in to her setting routine once more and Peter gets ready to take his shot. Suddenly the cock pheasant breaks out and he is up and off giving a bit of a crow out of himself, as he gets airborne. We are looking at all of this from the bottom of the field. We see the pheasant take off ten yards in front of Peter. We see him put the gun to his shoulder, see the smoke leave the end of his barrels, hear the two shots go off and see the pheasant fly on untouched. We have all missed easy birds like this before; it is part of the fun. But Peter made it even funnier. Having missed the bird he flings his shotgun onto the ground and starts jumping up and down on it. I don't think that any of us ever laughed more than we did that winter's afternoon down in Carlow with the Two Billys and after a good lunch in the Tobanstown Inn.

* * *

The summons, when it eventually arrived, demanded my presence in Naas district court on 23 December 1982. At this stage I was receiving quite a lot of 'free' legal aid from my good friends in the legal business and some kind of constitutional challenge along the lines of the McGee case was being mooted. If we could have established that Mr Sheridan's constitutional rights to privacy were being violated then such a course would have the effect of my being acquitted and the law being declared unconstitutional thus killing two birds with the one stone. But since Mr Sheridan was not married at the time this seemed to weaken our case. Anyway, the upshot of the whole thing was that when 23 December came along, we asked for and received an adjournment thus winning a six-month stay of execution.

Our next outing to Naas district court took place on Monday, 22 June 1983. By this time we had decided that an appeal to the High Court on constitutional grounds was too risky, too expensive and would be too long drawn out. We wanted the law on the sale of condoms to be changed quickly and the best way to achieve that was to run the case and embarrass the government as much as possible. The case was to be heard in front of Justice Johnston and I was to defend myself. The only danger here was that I would be found guilty but given the Probation Act. That, after all, would have been a perfectly reasonable course for Justice Johnston to take given that this was my first offence. Had that happened we would have been left dead in the water and the whole thing would have been a bit of a damp squib. Here again I had a bit of luck on my side.

The state solicitor Mr Coonan, in the course of his cross-examination of Mr Sheridan, asked him what he wanted the condoms for. This quite extraordinary question caused a titter of laughter to go around the courthouse much to the clear annoyance of Your Honour. Things were going from bad to worse and it was my turn next. The state solicitor then asked me why I thought it necessary to break the law. This set me off on a diatribe on how ridiculous I felt the law was and how it was unworkable and so on. I was just getting into second gear when Justice Johnston abruptly interrupted me asking that I desist immediately and sit down and that he would not have 'his court' used by anyone to score political points. And there I was thinking that the courts belonged to the people.

Clearly very annoyed, which was just how we needed him to be, the judge then asked Mr Coonan what the maximum fine was that he could impose. After a bit of thumb-licking through the statutes the state solicitor came back with the answer that I already knew to be the case: '£500, Your Honour.'

'Right,' says Justice Johnston, '£500 it is then or twenty-eight days in prison in default of payment.'

I could have applauded the judge and the state solicitor right there and then only that I thought it might be churlish to do so. But this was exactly the result that I wanted and Your Honour had played a blinder.

Outside, in front of several TV and media cameras, I said that I felt it quite extraordinary that a doctor should be fined £500 for practising medicine according to his conscience, that what happened inside the court-room just now was the natural consequences of Mr Haughey's so-called Irish solution to the Irish problem, that I would continue to sell condoms directly to people where I thought that such action was appropriate and that I would rot in prison before I would pay one penny of a fine that I believed to be wholly unjust – all very bullish stuff.

At this stage we had the option of leaving it at that, of not appealing against conviction or fine, not paying the fine and putting it up to the state to imprison me. This way I would have been the only doctor ever to be imprisoned for selling a package of ten condoms and embarrassment to the government would have been considerable. But there were a number of potential flaws to this approach. My wife and family were naturally hesitant and apprehensive about it, there was always the danger that some 'third party' would pay the fine on my behalf thus killing the whole thing off and in any event we had made our point and enough was enough. Taking all this into consideration the prevailing wisdom was to keep the thing alive and to appeal.

My final invitation to appear at Naas district court came a few months later and on 7 December of that same year I appeared before Mr Justice Frank Roe on appeal. At this hearing I asked a colleague, Dr Derek Freedman, a consultant in sexually transmitted diseases, to give evidence on my behalf. After a lengthy hearing during which we were given every chance to make our case Judge Roe summed up the whole thing as 'a storm in a teacup'. By this he meant that if people needed condoms in the evening or over a weekend when the local pharmacy shop might be closed then all they need do was to exercise some restraint and 'wait until Monday'.

He gave me the Probation Act on the grounds that it was my first offence, the fine was lifted and that was that. Nearly all the papers the next day bore headlines based on 'Wait Until Monday'. Some months later Justice Frank Roe, who was himself a keen amateur jockey, named one of his horses 'Wait Until Monday' which showed that the man at least had some sense of humour if not a very profound grasp of human sexual behaviour. The horse did quite well too.

I had many friends and great support throughout all of this farce. Dr Paddy Leahy and Dr Jim Loughran were both GPs who had pioneered for the kind of human rights that I was now campaigning for many years before I came on the plot. They and many other GP colleagues supported me all the way. The Irish Family Planning Association was incredibly supportive notwithstanding the fact that it would lose out financially in the event of condoms becoming more freely available. To this day I have a drawer full of letters of support from all over Ireland and indeed all over the world. I had my detractors too, of course, but they were in the minority. One lady from Birmingham sent me a package of used condoms asking if this was the kind of filth that I wanted to bring into Ireland.

In any case what matters is that it worked. Within a few weeks of the Roe hearing the now minister for Health, Barry Desmond, asked for a meeting with us, the directors of the IFPA, to explore our views on his proposed amendments to the Family Planning Act. These were to virtually deregulate the sale of condoms making them freely available through chemists' shops and vending machines in men's public toilets. During this meeting I mentioned to the minister that I was on probation for selling a package of condoms. The minister replied that he was fully aware of that fact and that this gave a certain urgency to these proposed new amendments. Within a few weeks they were written into law and that was that.

What I did through this deliberate act of civil disobedience was to bring about change to Mr Haughey's Irish solution to an Irish problem and make condoms available to those who wanted them without the need for seeing a doctor. I have no doubt but that these changes would have come along anyway sooner or later. But knowing the nature of these things and the Irish government's built-in resistance to grasping certain nettles it would have been later rather than sooner.

* * *

By this time I had a fairly good family practice built up and I had been brought into the medical card or GMS scheme. By and large I was single-handed which made the going a bit rough at times. Also I was on call for too many nights and weekends and was finding it very difficult to get away. The telephone answering machine I remember was a great invention for the hard-pressed single-handed rural GP. At least now you did not need to have someone sitting by the phone all day. The mobile or cellular phone, when it eventually arrived in 1984, was to revolutionise general practice. Now with a message on the answering machine giving out a mobile number, a doctor on call was relatively free to move about.

I still missed the hospital work and the better working and paying conditions of Canada. There were far too many demands for unnecessary house calls and it was very difficult to stop people coming to my hall door on a Sunday afternoon and enquiring if I was 'on duty'. It may have been around this time too that I began to understand the concept of having a 'vocation' for general practice. My tolerance for people making unreasonable demands outside of surgery hours was not without limits and I know that I was often impatient with people and their insistence that I respond to their every whim. These stresses too I have no doubt did very little to improve my floundering marriage.

Many of my colleagues did not share with me this tetchiness or intolerance of people's unreasonable demands or if they did they never showed it. At some level I envied them and their enormous practices which being nice all the time can bring. At another level though I wondered about their sanity and the quality of their family and personal lives. Doctors are first and foremost fallible human beings with feelings the same as anyone else. Not allowing oneself give vent to those feelings on the basis of being the possessor of a vocation could be positively bad for one's health.

To compensate for all of these things of course I had my vasectomy practice within the Irish Family Planning Association and within my own general practice in Clane. The nice thing about doing a vasectomy is that there is a beginning, middle and an end. A lot of the time in general practice this is not the case. An old woman is lonely and fearsome and depressed. She worries about dying and is short of breath. At night in bed her legs feel hot and she has noticed too that she is getting dizzy spells. Her eldest son is an alcoholic, her husband passed away four years ago with lung cancer. She has a pain in her left hand and she has been out of tablets for three days. The consultation has no beginning and certainly no end. Somewhere in there there may be a middle. But this is hard going when you have no vocation.

If someone comes into my surgery with a broken arm and a deep laceration to the forehead I am brilliant, I know exactly what to do and I will have them all fixed up in a minute. But if the same person should come in with a broken heart I am useless. Do not talk to me either about how awful your marriage is. I have a bad marriage myself and don't know what to do about it. I must have been the worst marriage counsellor in Ireland. If your marriage were in some difficulty before you discussed it with me, it would be much worse after your visit. My idea of marriage counselling was to blame whichever party was not present during the consultation.

I also had my writing. At first I wrote a weekly column for the *Irish Medical Times* and later moved over to writing for the *Irish Medical News* to which I still contribute regularly. Not only did this bring in an extra few shillings but also more importantly I think they allowed me to vent my feelings on a lot of topics as diverse as abortion, euthanasia, suicide and alternative medicine. Writing to a deadline is a good discipline; it forces one to assemble one's thoughts in a logical order and demands accuracy and accountability.

* * *

Up in Allenwood South a young man is squatted down behind his house trying to have a bowel movement. It is a small house but a neat one. He is surrounded by mushrooms of green milky froth. He is crying and occasionally lets a roar out of him. He is going to die and I can do nothing for him. I am a doctor, he is dying and I can do nothing for him. Young men trying to help him to vomit surround him. I can smell the Paraquat all around this place; its hideous green stain is mixed up with the milk that the squatting man has managed to vomit up.

How much of it did he take, I want to know. A young woman beside me says that she saw him drink a full cupful. One teaspoonful of Paraquat will kill you and everyone around the squatting man knows that and he knows it too and that is why he is roaring and crying and trying to have a bowel movement and vomit but it is too late. He is staring death straight in the face and death stares grimly back at him. He is already dying and he will be dead within a few days. The Paraquat has now gone into his bloodstream and is making its deadly way to his kidneys and to his liver and to his brain and every organ it touches will be completely destroyed and there will be nothing left. A vacuum. But most importantly of all the Paraquat is going to his lungs and this is where it will do its greatest damage in the shortest space of time. Tomorrow he will have gross pulmonary oedema and respiratory failure, the next day he will be on a respirator and the next day he will be dead because they will switch off the respirator as there is no point in going on.

Why did the squatting man drink a cupful of Paraquat? He drank it because he had a row with his girlfriend and he wanted to show her. Show her what I never knew.

* * *

Running parallel with the condom debacle was the 'pro-life amendment campaign'. Ever since the pope's visit to Ireland in 1979 a certain large section of the population had been whipping itself up into a renewed religious fervour and looking for a cause. The subject of abortion seemed like an obvious one. Abortion was already illegal in Ireland at the time but the pro-life amendment people wanted more. They wanted to make it doubly illegal by enshrining – to use their word – into the Irish constitution an amendment that would make any attempt at reversing the law prohibiting abortion unconstitutional. This they told us would copper-fasten – again their word – a prohibition on abortion in Ireland for all time. Thus they said Ireland would become like a shining beacon to the rest of the world as a unique place that respected and cherished all human life from the moment of conception. Others of us pointed out that:

- Abortion was unfortunately innate to the human species with examples of the practice going back in history for as long as history will take us.
- That history, including recent Irish history, will show that where there is no access to legal abortion there will be illegal or so-called back-street abortion and baby abandonment.
- That since we were currently exporting our abortion requirements to England at a rate of 5,000 per year any talk of us being a shining beacon was a tad hypocritical.
- That there was no place on this earth that had a zero rate of abortion nor any example of any place in the world where abortion was successfully 'stamped out'.

The first thing that those of us opposed to the pro-life amendment learned was that if you were against them then that automatically made you anti-life and pro-abortion. It was this kind of smearing that made the whole debate so terribly divisive, vicious and unpleasant. The issues and the way that the debate was constructed were destined to divide families and friends then and for a long time afterwards. Because of my position as chairman of the Irish Family Planning Association and the attention received by my opposition to the Condom Act I was invited to many meetings all around the country to speak on the anti-amendment side.

It was always a lost cause. People were going to vote yes 'to save babies' lives', yes 'to keep Ireland abortion free', yes 'to life'. The fact that a yes vote did not necessarily mean any of these things was lost and in any case the priest from the altar had asked them to vote 'yes' and wasn't that good enough for anyone? The pro-life people had God on their side and they were firmly dug into the high moral ground. They won by a very comfortable majority but eventually it was to be a hollow victory.

The eighth amendment to the constitution was passed and it read:

> *The state acknowledges the right to life of the unborn and, with due regard to the equal right to life of the mother, guarantees in its laws to respect, and, as far as practicable, by its laws to defend and vindicate that right.*

Nine years later the inevitable happened. A fourteen-year-old girl became pregnant as a result of rape. Mr Justice Costello granted a High Court injunction preventing her from travelling to the UK for an abortion. This caused a public outcry and the case was appealed to the Supreme Court. There, three days later and by the narrowest of majorities, the injunction was lifted. The judges took the view that in this case there was a substantive risk to the life of the mother since she had threatened suicide and therefore a termination would not be unlawful and she should be allowed to travel. This became known as the X case and it totally undermined the pro-lifers' Eighth Amendment. So much for enshrining, copper-fastening and beacons of light.

The situation now is that by Supreme Court precedent abortion in Ireland is not illegal where there is a substantial risk to the life of the mother. But there is no matching legislation and the government has repeatedly said that they have no plans to revisit this most contentious of subjects. The matter stands in abeyance and the numbers of Irish women travelling to the UK every year for abortions has fallen slightly in the last two years. That at least is good news.

* * *

I cannot say for sure if this woman is beautiful or not. I suspect that she is beautiful. Her eyes are beautiful, deep brown and almond-shaped. But the rest is hidden. I cannot make out her face because it is hidden behind her boshiya. She is tall and probably slim but I am not sure. Her body is in there somewhere within the voluminous folds of her thobe, which in turn is covered by her large black cloak called an abaya. Her clinical records tell me that fourteen different general practitioners have seen her over the last sixteen months. These notes also tell me that two years ago she lost a six-month-old baby and that more recently her husband has taken a second wife. She is on Valium, 10 mg three times a day. I can feel her pain.

I am in Saudi Arabia for two months because they will not let us build our hospital back home. The plans are drawn up; the money is in, the company incorporated. Kildare county council have granted permission but a local schoolteacher has appealed against the permission to An Bord Pleanála. This will hold us up for at least another year. It may even scuttle the whole project. The schoolteacher's objections are 'constitutional'. Because we foolishly mentioned female sterilisation in our articles of association this objector is now claiming that since the Irish constitution affords protection to the family and since being sterilised is somehow anti-family then the proposed hospital is 'unconstitutional'. It matters not one bit that this objection is utterly spurious and fallacious. The quality of the objection is not the point. Any objection to An Bord Pleanála at that time had to go through due process and had the effect of delaying development for at least one year.

I had to get away or I was going to go mad. My marriage was going nowhere and the hospital was going nowhere. The pro-lifers had captured the high moral ground with their Eighth Amendment and it was time to get away for a while. Saudi Arabia was looking for general practitioners to work in their hospitals on short-term contracts of two months and this seemed like an ideal opportunity to do something completely different, to gather my thoughts and to regroup.

The hospital that I was assigned to was in a city called Khamis Mushait close to the Yemeni border and the Red Sea, in the southwest of the kingdom. The best thing that I can say about Khamis Mushait is that it is situated 3,000 feet above sea level and therefore enjoys a Mediterranean-like climate most of the year round. Thus at least we were spared the stultifying heat and humidity suffered by our colleagues in cities like Jeddah and Riyadh.

Our group of some ten general practitioners was housed in a compound like a small old-fashioned housing estate. There was about an equal mix of men and women, three of us were from Ireland. The minibus arrived every morning at eight o'clock to take us to work in the GP section of the large King Fahad Military Hospital a couple of miles away. This was an artificial 'practice' grafted onto a hospital which reflected the fact that Saudi did not have many indigenous general practices on the ground. I did not think that this was a good idea at all at the time and indeed I suspect that by now the Saudi authorities will have spotted the limitations of this approach to the delivery of community health.

When Saudi suddenly became extremely oil rich they set about building state of the art infrastructures like hospitals, medical schools and clinics, from which to deliver a healthcare service for the people. Mistakes of course were made and one of them was to graft general practice onto hospitals to be staffed by overseas doctors and then to invite the people to go in and get some health advice. This was a disaster and I know because I worked at the coalface of this system for two months and can honestly say that I never saw one *bona fide* sick person in all my time there. Not one. Everyone coming in to see these overseas doctors had an agenda that had nothing to do with medicine. And what made it all worse was that doctor and pseudo-patient spoke different languages and came from cultures that were poles apart. This was a total mess and a charade.

All consultations had to be conducted through an interpreter. This in itself was a massive barrier and frankly unworkable. Take for example lovely eyes sitting here before me now. Her life is a total mess and now to make matters worse she is addicted to the Valium that my previous colleagues kept giving her. This is all wrong; this is bad doctoring and bad medicine. As a doctor I would love to help her to work through her pain and find some resolution or some closure. This would take a lot of time, trust in each other and dialogue. But there is no dialogue, no trust and no continuity of care.

I ask the interpreter if she would ask the lady behind the boshiya how she feels about her husband having recently taken a second wife. The interpreter, herself a Jordanian Muslim, turns to me and most emphatically says that she cannot ask that kind of question and suggests that I give the lady a repeat prescription for Valium and let's get on with it. Now my confusion is complete. Is the subject of a woman's feelings about a second wife really a taboo subject? Or is it only taboo because I am asking another female to put the question to the lady in the thobe. Or is it that the interpreter is in a hurry to get home and would prefer not to be bothered engaging with the beautiful eyes across the desk. I do not know the answers to any of these questions. I am completely out of my depth here. All I do know is that from there on in the interpreter ran the show. I practised medicine in Saudi Arabia in a way that would have had me rightly struck off the register if I were back in Ireland. The patients got their medicines and nobody got any better. In two months' time another bunch of GPs would arrive and the cycle would be repeated.

During our time off, and we had a lot of time off, we sat around a swimming pool at our compound or we played tennis or otherwise just chilled out. The only problem with the swimming pool was that there was no water in it. All the water drained away months earlier and they could not find anyone capable of fixing it. That was typical of the place at the time. When things broke down they just stayed that way. Know-how and craftsmanship were thin on the ground. The place was full of chiefs but very few Indians. But the empty pool did not bother me all that much since I do not swim.

What did bother me though and what bothered most of us was the total lack of alcohol. I suppose the fact that none of us got the DTs on day five off alcohol suggests that none of us were alcoholics in the classic sense but frankly that was not much consolation. But a little help was at hand. After about ten days there I had struck up a warm relationship with a colleague and she and I sussed out a small private speakeasy in town run by Americans working for McDonald Douglas. Here they served sadeki red or white in plastic cups. Sadeki is an illicit alcohol drink made from fermented grape juice and available, to those in the know, all over the Arab world. It's a bit like reasonably good plonk but that did not matter. It was the fact that we were breaking the law and beating the system that made the whole thing so hilarious. Now we knew what fun people must have had during the prohibition in America in the 1920s.

Of course we had to be careful. European doctors and Americans were generally left alone but only within reason. Any drunken disorderliness on our behalf would not have been tolerated. The hospital authorities held our passports as security against bad behaviour and it was hard to escape the feeling that one was being constantly watched. But we survived and all in all I have to say that my sojourn in Saudi Arabia was a very interesting one. As doctors we may not have been able to bring much succour to the people but that was only because 'the system' got in the way. I returned from that place £4,000 the richer and within weeks of coming home An Bord Pleanála overruled the moral objections and finally we could start to build our little hospital.

CHAPTER 10

Clane General Hospital

Up to and during my term as chairman of the Irish Family Planning Association in the early 1980s there were no facilities in Dublin where a woman could go for a tubal ligation if that was what she wished to do. Someone seeking female sterilisation up to this time had to, in the main, go to the UK. There was a small private hospital down in Cork where a limited number of tubal ligations or TLs were being carried out but the gynaecologist working there, Dr Edgar Ritchie, was anxious to limit the numbers lest the hospital assume the mantle of a 'sterilisation clinic'. His reservations were very understandable. So whereas by this time we had male sterilisation up and running in Ireland for well over a decade, the female equivalent was almost unavailable. The reason why this was the case was because male sterilisation or vasectomy is a straightforward procedure requiring just a doctor's surgery setting, a local anaesthetic and one operator, female sterilisation or TL, on the other hand, is a far more complex procedure requiring a hospital setting, a general anaesthetic and a team of doctors and nurses all free of scruples or hang-ups about doing something not approved of by the Holy Roman Catholic Church. And that in fact was the single biggest barrier that we encountered in trying to establish a female sterilisation facility in Ireland – getting a team together that was not cowed by Roman dictate.

A number of avenues were explored. An existing nursing home would have been an obvious choice. We did not need x-ray or laboratory facilities nor did we need huge sophistication in terms of operating theatre technology. By adding on basic operating or surgery facilities to an existing nursing home and designating about six beds to that unit you would have what we needed. With this in mind I approached the proprietors of a number of Dublin nursing homes and one in Kildare. While they all gave my proposition due and often positive consideration, when they worked out the logistics of the whole thing they politely declined. It soon became apparent to me that if we were going to establish a centre for female sterilisation in Ireland it was not going to happen via the 'existing nursing homes' idea.

That left me with only two alternatives. Either I should build a new facility somewhere or perhaps I could buy some existing facility like a guesthouse and convert it into what was needed. At this stage my horizons were expanding. Building a small hospital to do TLs alone clearly was not a viable proposition since, as time went on and more people were offering the same service, we could not reasonable expect to survive on this alone. Knowing this it became clear that what I should do was to build a small general hospital that offered female sterilisation along with all the other medical, obstetrical and surgical disciplines appropriate to such a setting. And thus was born the concept of what is today, twenty years later, Clane General Hospital, with some fifty visiting consultants, a staff of over one hundred good people and an annual turnover in excess of five million euro and rising.

Looking at it today with its new extensions and expanded diagnostic facilities, people often come up to me and say something nice like: 'Wasn't it very far-sighted of you to start off this hospital and aren't you the great fellow altogether?' I just smile and thank the person for saying such kind things. But the fact of the matter is that there was nothing particularly far-sighted about any of it. It was more to do with muddling along, lurching from crisis to crisis and hoping for the best. It was in fact, and we used to say it to each other at the time, a big leap into the darkness. And in any case, for the first four or five years of our existence we were too busy trying to just survive and had very little time to be gazing into the future or being far-sighted. And it was an absolute nightmare that brought me as close to utter ruination as I ever want to go and did nothing at all to save my floundering marriage. I made lots of mistakes of course. But then to be fair about it I didn't have any models to guide me.

Mistake number one for example: I never drew up a business plan. Nobody ever told me that I might need one. But had I done, it might have gone some way towards avoiding the stonewall of cash-flow problems that we hit six months after opening the place and struggled with for another two years. And besides that a good and honest business plan would have forced me to see what the minimum number of consultants was that would need to be committed to the place before we could press the 'go' button.

Establishing a private hospital is completely different to say establishing a four-star hotel. People choose to go to a hotel and to stay there for as long or for as short a time as they like. They do this of their own volition. If they like the place they may come back and stay again the following year. If they really like the place they may tell their friends about it. None of this applies to a hospital. People by and large do not choose which hospital they go to. Their own GP and the consultant they are referred to generally make this choice for them. Neither do you decide how long you would like to stay in a hospital but rather this is decided for you by whatever is the matter with you or what sort of operation you have had. By and large hospitals do not do a lot of 'repeat business'. You stay there once, you get fixed up and you hope to never see the place again. Neither does word of mouth do much for a hospital although it is of course important to have a good professional reputation and to hold on to it.

The key to starting up a private hospital is to first of all identify a group of well-established and popular consultants who you think might be committed to the new venture. Ideally these consultants should hold a public appointment and should be prepared to become tied into the venture financially. These consultants will already have established a rapport with a large group of GPs who will continue to refer patients to them. These consultants, GPs and their patients then become the natural media in which to grow a thriving hospital.

When I started Clane Hospital I did not have nearly enough committed and established consultants, I simply did not have enough of this natural medium or the bedrock on which to build a hospital. My failure to attract such consultants may have had a lot to do with my being a GP, as distinct from a consultant. And of course my reputation of being something of a radical did not help either. Medicine is traditionally a deeply conservative profession and many doctors then and even today tend to give mavericks a wide berth or indeed resent their very existence.

But even before this I had made mistakes or was badly advised. As already mentioned, in our memorandum and articles of association we stated that we intended to do female sterilisation at Clane General Hospital. This was a bad mistake. There was absolutely no need or any legal requirement for us to have specified TL as one of the surgical procedures that were to be carried out at Clane Hospital. What mentioning this in our articles did was to give ammunition to a third party objector to An Bord Pleanála who appealed Kildare county council's permission as soon as it was granted. This nearly put us out of business before we started.

During the time I was in Saudi and while we were awaiting An Bord Pleanála's decision on the 'constitutional objection', just up the road from us in Celbridge a colleague, Dr Gerry Waters, announced to an eager press that he was about to open a centre where female sterilisation would be available. It was to be a simple dedicated unit with overnight facilities that he was to call the Whitethorn Clinic. On a regular basis a London consultant would be flown in to carry out tubal ligations in this clinic. This was not good news for us. We had been relying on these very operations to prime our planned hospital and here it now looked as though Gerry had stolen the march on us. Of course looking back on all of this now none of it really mattered all that much as things turned out, it was just that at the time they seemed so terribly important. In any case our company had been formed, investors had come in and the land purchased and at this stage we had little choice but to forge ahead.

When An Bord Pleanála eventually confirmed planning permission on 8 January 1985 we wasted little time in starting what we liked to think of as 'phase one' of Clane General Hospital. At this particular time there was a serious lull in the building trade so it was relatively easy to get builders and to ensure that they stuck to their task. Thus it was that we had the first part of the hospital, with its small out-patients department, administrative offices, fourteen beds, x-ray department, physiotherapy department, operating theatre, anaesthetic and recovery rooms, all finished and kitted out within eight months of starting the project. On 24 August of that same year, with about twenty local GPs, media and other well-wishers in attendance, Fine Gael TD Monica Barnes officially opened the place for us. That was a good day.

Things limped along all right for the rest of that year. We had a fair backlog of tubal ligations to work through, a cosmetic surgeon started to do some work and our co-director and investor, Mr Robin Mooney, was bringing in a trickle of surgical cases. I was administrator, chairman of the board of directors and had moved my general practice into offices annexed to the hospital. But by the following spring it was becoming clear that we were facing a serious cash-flow problem. Later that year the shareholders had to make additional investments on several occasions in order to keep ourselves afloat and on one occasion I had to sell my car to pay the nurses' wages. As is often the case in situations like these there was a lot of blaming and most of it was coming in my direction. For example my having a general practice located in the hospital was perceived as a prime reason why GPs were slow to refer patients to Clane and why more consultants were not joining us. It was difficult to ascertain to what extent, if any, this theory was correct. It may well have had some validity but equally there undoubtedly was something of making me the fall guy as well.

That year also an old medical school friend of mine, Dr Billy Byrne, came up with the suggestion that he and I set up a company to carry out clinical trials on behalf of the international pharmaceutical industry. We called the company International Medical Research (IMR) and entered into an agreement with the hospital to use their beds and ancillary facilities in the event of our winning contracts for such clinical trials.

That second year also further disaster struck when we had an anaesthetic death. A middle-aged lady undergoing a facelift never came round from the anaesthetic and died three days later. This kind of thing tragically can happen in any hospital but we were particularly vulnerable to the adverse publicity that came in its wake. This was by way of front-page coverage in the *Sunday Independent* – one of Ireland's most popular Sunday newspapers. They used a large photograph of me to accompany the 'story' even though I was neither surgeon nor anaesthetist. I had to take the full brunt of blame in the public eye. I remember the night before this news broke neither Ann nor I slept a wink because we knew what was coming. That Sunday afternoon we were at a bit of a get-together where I met a colleague of mine, Dr Ralph Counahan, who went out of his way to commiserate with us and to shore us up a bit in what must have been one of our most miserable hours. He may never have known just how important those few words were to me at that precise time. Poor Ralph died himself a few years later.

The clinical trials end of things in fact went quite well and IMR won a few simple 'bio-availability' studies that brought some business to the hospital. We also did a private placing of twenty-five per cent of IMR shares, raising a very respectable quarter of a million pounds through Davy Stockbrokers. One would imagine that this might have calmed nerves all around but in fact it did the exact opposite. The modest success of IMR brought out the begrudgery factor in some of my co-directors in the hospital who now began to look on IMR, not as a potential saviour, but rather as a threat. There were 'meetings' in the car park, in the corridors and down in Manzor's pub in Clane but I was not at any of them. Earlier I had been relieved of my position as hospital administrator – a good move on behalf of my fellow directors because I was not particularly good at the job that, by this time, consisted mostly of batting off creditors. But soon I was to be voted off the chair of the board, something that I took to be pure vindictiveness. A little later I was forced by the board of the hospital to relocate my general practice out of the hospital altogether. These were turbulent days.

But the human spirit is strong. Gradually things settled down and some of the more truculent doctors resigned or otherwise drifted off with themselves and we brought in a new and more 'neutral' chairman, Jim Canning, who also brought along a few very welcome new investors. But most importantly of all more consultants were now beginning to take an interest in the place and my replacement CEO, Seán Leyden, along with his wife, Gladys, who was and still is, director of nursing, steadied the ship and we were beginning to head for calmer waters. In fact within five years of opening the hospital we were at least solvent and in a position to start building our phase two development. This consisted of an additional twenty-five-bed wing of private and semi-private rooms, a new and expanded x-ray and ultrasound department, a new physiotherapy and sports-injury department and a suite of seven additional consulting-rooms. We were getting there.

* * *

Dawn comes slowly over the South Slobs in Wexford. My good dog Jet is beside me in my hide shivering slightly and looking out over the brackish water. She is there to retrieve shot ducks. We are lucky to have been drawn for the Tongue Gate where hundreds of teal are stirring themselves. There is a decent wind up with spits of rain mixed into it. This is good wildfowling weather. Teal, when they have a tail wind behind them, can travel at speeds in excess of fifty miles an hour. Shooting does not get any more challenging than this. I can hear their wings cut through the air, as they turn high overhead. But I can't see them properly yet; Jet and I must wait for more light.

It is 6.45 on this mid-December Sunday morning. Soon the winter sun staggers along the horizon like a drunken man reluctant to make a proper appearance. Now I can just about make out my surroundings. The tall reeds on each side of the channel are copper and gold. The water is shimmering silver. I can see the blinds 300 metres across the channel from me in the reeds of the Pill of Ray. A gun, Jack-in-the-box fashion, mans each hide. The fellows over there all work in the AIB. We call them the A team. All is still. A coot calls from somewhere and a reed warbler warbles.

Now I catch a glimpse of three teal heading my way and about to cross high right to left twenty-five yards out from our blind. I bend low in the hide and press the safety catch forwards with my thumb. The dog is looking at the birds and back at me. She is deeply suspicious of the outcome for she has seen me miss so many times. In two seconds I am up and onto them. I pick out the leading duck. To kill a bird going this fast you have to catch up with him first, them get ahead of him by a good ten feet and then, and this is the bit we all forget, you do not stop the gun but keep it sweeping forwards of your target all the time. For a change I seem to have done all the right things this time because when I squeeze the trigger the teal tumbles in the air feet up and comes crashing into the reeds thirty yards off to my left.

The dog is away. There were no whistles, no hand-signals, and no 'good dog, fetch up'. She dives in and is away of her own volition. She has seen where the bird has fallen and it is all down to herself from here on. Deep inside the tall reeds I can hear her splashing about. The tops of the reeds shimmy to her movements below and then suddenly there is silence and stillness. Every wildfowler knows this moment.

The black Labrador has stopped moving inside the reeds. But has she stopped because she has lost interest or has she stopped to pick up the small bird? In two minutes she is swimming towards me with the teal held in her soft mouth in the water in front of her. This is the miracle and the wonder of wildfowling. Not that a man can shoot a bird but that a dog can then go and find it. No human being can do that. And best of all the bankers across the channel have seen all this and I feel so proud, not for myself at shooting a difficult teal but for my good dog Jet for finding it.

CHAPTER 11

The End of a Marriage

At this stage I have been relegated to the bedroom haunted by Alice Aylmer, the jilted wife of the last Bury of Downings. I had been in there for the last three months and was to stay there for another two years until I eventually came to terms with my broken marriage and quit the house altogether. I have only three bits of advice for you if your marriage runs into difficulty, advice that I spectacularly ignored, of course, in my own case. Firstly, do not ask yourself 'what will people think of me?' because the question is totally irrelevant. What people think of you and your marital breakdown is neither here nor there and utterly unimportant. Your first duty is, as always, towards yourself.

When I was first trying to come to terms with marital breakdown I was in denial. And when considering moving out and into, for example, an apartment, I wondered what my patients would think of me and would my practice suffer. In actual fact my patients could not care less if I was living at home or on the far side of the moon but that is not the point. The point is that I was very stupid to be asking the question in the first place.

The second piece of advice is to either end it or mend it but do not just ignore it because it will most certainly not go away. Nor will it 'come right in time'. Again in this department I was quite pathetic. When I look back at it now I wonder just what was I thinking about when sleeping in that spare bedroom for almost two and a half years. Did I really think that that was normal or that one day things would, as it were, right themselves?

And lastly of course talk your problems over with a trusted friend or confidante and share the problem with your offspring in a non-threatening way. I never told a sinner that my marriage was foundering nor did I let any of my children, then in their late teens and early twenties, in on the true situation. Now I think that was a mistake.

* * *

The man smoking the pipe is a psychiatrist and a marriage counsellor. He is a small neat man in his mid-forties. We are in this big room in this old hospital called St Pat's. At the first hour-long session he speaks to both of us together and tries to come to some understanding as to why it is that we are not getting along and why are we making ourselves generally miserable. The next two sessions are individual ones, one for Ann, followed by one for me. The last hour-long session is for both of us. This was a fairly standard couple-counselling format.

It is tempting to say that the marriage counselling was no use and a waste of time or that our therapist was inept and unhelpful. The fact of the matter was that our relationship was as dead as a duck and there was little point in expecting miracles. What these sessions did do was make us focus in on our relationship problem and to respect the legitimacy of the other's point of view. While this didn't save the marriage it did nonetheless take a lot of the heat out of the situation and rows and arguments became practically a thing of the past. After about another year both of us were ready to move on to the next step, to mediation and separation. The gig was up and the die cast.

* * *

I was driving home from work and listening to a man being interviewed on the radio. The man was a retired Irish army officer who had served some time out in Namibia and was now organising groups of Irish to take two weeks travelling on safaris in that strange and very beautiful land. The way the retired officer was describing the place made it seem so interesting and attractive. They gave out his phone number after the programme and I took careful note of it. I wanted to have a look at Namibia.

Actually there was another reason for my wanting to travel other than to look at the giraffes and baboons of southwest Africa. With total marital breakdown finally acknowledged and mediation counselling entered into I was, as it were, on the market or at least certainly did not cherish the prospect of living out the rest of my life alone. Perhaps then I might meet someone interesting among this group of forty Irish thrill-seekers. But if that's what I thought then a quick look around the departure lounge where we mustered before takeoff very quickly quenched any vague notions I may have been harbouring about Africa, romance and safari. They were a lovely diverse bunch of people, many indeed with problems of their own but future partner potential? I hardly thought so.

A few days after returning from Namibia I was having a pint with Billy Byrne in O'Brien's of Leeson Street, a famous old Dublin pub with wooden floors and old-fashioned layout. In the pub at the same time were Joan Morrissey and her friend, Dee Ryan. Billy knew both of these ladies to see and we got chatting to them. The upshot of the whole thing anyway was that I stayed up more or less all night talking to the two women. Within a few weeks of this chance encounter I packed my things, moved out of Downings and started to live with Joan in Ballsbridge. After my separation a few years later I bought back Ann's share in Downings House and returned to live there with Joan who I married a few years later and everyone lived more or less happily ever after. It is funny how things have a way of working themselves out, painful and all as it may have been for all involved at the time.

* * *

I caught my first salmon on the Moy river when I had just turned sixty-two years of age. The Moy river rises high in the Ox mountains, swings down through Foxford before heading due north through Ballina and on out to the sea in Killala Bay. The Moy is not an enormous river but it just so happens to be one of the finest salmon fishing rivers in Europe, if not in fact the finest one. It is fished for nearly all of its length but the most popular places are in the town of Ballina itself. As you cross the bridge leaving the town the Ridge pool is on your right-hand side and the Cathedral pool is on your left. The Ridge pool is an icon in the world of salmon fishing. Since I am very new to this sport and my friends want me to catch my first salmon before I die they very wisely take me to the place where my chances of doing so are at their greatest. At my age there is little point in wasting time.

We pull in and get out of the car to take a look. This place is pure street theatre. All along the length of the river on both sides people lean over the wall and watch the anglers down below as they strut their stuff. They have for the most part waded out into the middle of the river up to their waists and higher in the water. Every ten or fifteen seconds a salmon leaps clear. These are all big fish. Most impressive of all are those who use the long double-handled fly rods. These are used to 'spay cast' which is a sideward action as distinct from the more usual overhead casting technique. In one smooth movement they haul their long floating line out of the water and bring it back up beside them in a loop before casting it out once more across the flow of the river. As the long line turns before making its outwards journey it emits a loud 'swish' and a whip-crack sound. It then follows a dead straight and tight journey to gently drop the sinking fly thirty yards away. I do not know how they do this but I could watch them all day. This is all art and drama tied up in one.

Over dinner I complained to my friends that this stuff is way beyond my new-found skills as a fly-fisherman and that perhaps it was a mistake for me to have come here. First of all I hate wading in strong currents and always feel that I am going to fall over at any second. Then there is the matter of not owning or knowing how to use a two-handed rod. And thirdly I did not relish the thoughts of having a large audience leaning over the bridge watching me flounder around in the river below them. But my friends just ignored me and said I'd be fine, that my single-handed rod would do grand and the current wasn't that strong and there would be nobody looking at me and would I ever shut up and drink my wine.

We are on the Moy the next morning at six o'clock. When you are booked onto the Ridge pool there is no messing. Starting times are all to do with tides and I have exactly seven hours to catch my first salmon. They are jumping out of the water all over the place but the question is will they be interested in my poorly presented offerings. There are five rods on this stretch. You wade out into the middle of the river starting at the top beside the weir. After three or four casts you move down a few yards and proceed like this until you are down under the bridge at which stage you get out of the river, walk up to the top and start all over again. My friends were right – wading is not too bad. The riverbed is smooth and I can get a good grip on it, the current is manageable. I forget about falling in and my single-handed casting, while failing to draw a thunderous round of applause from the crowd up on the bridge, is nonetheless adequate. I am lost in what I am doing, too lost to care about extraneous matters like audience or style. Then suddenly BANG!

When you have a decent salmon on a single-handed rod you must make sure not to horse him but to let him run while always keeping in touch, never let your line slack but do not haul on it either. All my fishing companions on this stretch of the Moy are seasoned anglers and are well aware that I am only a doffer. But they kindly take me in. Soon a man is by my side with a landing net at the ready wanting to know if I have ever done this before. When I tell him that this is my first he is full of gratuitous advice and help. Anglers, like all proper sports people, help each other out. After about six minutes, during which time my salmon runs three times but never all that far, the fish flounders and I can lift his head out of the water. At this stage my helper slips the landing net under my catch and we have him on the bank, all five and a half pounds of him. This is a great country and thank you Mayo for my first real decent wild fish.

* * *

During my time living with Joan in Ballsbridge I became involved in a strange way with what was referred to then as the 'right to die' case. This was during the long hot summer of 1995. But I need to go back to the beginning.

Sometime during the spring of 1972 a bright and pretty young Dublin woman, well-educated and in the prime of her life, was suffering from painful periods or dysmenorrhoea as we call it in this profession. She was twenty-two years of age. About eighty per cent of all young women suffer from painful periods at some stage or other of their lives. Most of these women manage to keep going by taking something like Paracetamol for the first few days of their periods. In about ten per cent of young women however the degree of menstrual cramping can be so severe and incapacitating as to make it impossible for them to keep going and they may have to take to the bed or otherwise rest themselves holding a hot water bottle to their tummies. Thus they may have to miss out on school or work for a few days each month. Such young women therefore may need stronger treatment than simple over-the-counter analgesics. This young Dublin woman was such a case. She went to see her GP and he referred her to a conservative obstetrician gynaecologist. This was a bad mistake on behalf of the GP. Some GPs are in the habit of always playing it safe and referring anything more serious than the common head cold to specialists. Our young woman going to see a gynaecologist in April 1972 to treat her dysmenorrhoea was unwittingly heading towards catastrophe. The GP should have been able to treat her himself. This is not rocket science. The standard treatment for severe dysmenorrhoea back in 1972 was then, as it remains to this day, the oral contraceptive pill. By blocking ovulation you can stop painful periods in their tracks. You might think that this kind of treatment was 'too severe' but remember, if someone has menstrual cramps so severe as to render them incapable of going to school or work for two or three days a month, then treatments like the oral contraceptive pill are absolutely justifiable in the eyes of most reasonable doctors.

Unfortunately her GP did not take this view. Even as late as

1972 there was tremendous resistance among many Irish doctors to prescribing 'the pill' to unmarried women, particularly to sexually inactive unmarried young women. There was this ridiculous notion abroad that such prescribing could promote promiscuous behaviour. Whether it would or wouldn't is not the point and in fact is none of the doctor's business. The doctor's business is to treat the painful periods in the safest and most effective way possible. And prescribing the oral contraceptive pill is in most cases just such an approach. But our GP in this disastrous case flunked it and took the easy way out and kicked for touch. He decided to refer the young woman to a gynaecologist – a decision that was to have catastrophic consequences.

Gynaecologists operate. That is their stock-in-trade if you like, it is what they do. So the gynaecologist decided to perform a D&C on her. A D&C, or dilatation and curettage, is an operation on the womb where the cervix is dilated to allow an instrument inside to scrape away the womb's lining or endometrium. As a treatment for dysmenorrhoea, even back in 1972, it was already long outmoded, dangerous, ineffectual and totally inappropriate. But in this case it was to be much more than any of these things: death or, worse still, near death. She never recovered from the anaesthetic. During the operation she suffered from three cardiac arrests or heart stoppages. Each of these resulted in her brain being starved of oxygen for prolonged periods of time.

When the anaesthetic gases were eventually removed and efforts were made to bring her around she did not respond. Instead she lapsed into a deep coma or what is usually referred to as the 'persistent vegetative state' or PVS. To be strictly accurate about it in fact she was in a near-persistent vegetative state. Because she seemed to have glimmers of cognition in being able to perhaps recognise some of her long-term carers her condition was thought to be something slightly less than PVS. You might think that this was somehow good news. But it wasn't, quite the reverse in fact. It raised the possibility of her being vaguely aware of her predicament, which of course would have made her life intolerable. But things were to get even worse than that.

The poor girl's parents complained that they were given little or no explanation as to what had happened, why it had happened, what they were to expect or what the future would hold for their lovely daughter.

And so this once bright and beautiful young woman lay on a hospital bed sometimes on the flat of her back staring, perhaps unseeingly, up at the ceiling, totally paralysed and motionless except for her steady breathing and the darting movements of her eyes. Her carers had to turn her from one side onto the other to prevent her from developing pressure sores. She had no speech. She was unable to swallow. She could give no signal of thought or feeling other than an occasional despairing moan. She was trapped in her frozen world of deep unconsciousness, alive but unable to move, with no evidence of awareness of self or environment. Her wakeful unconsciousness had no real prospects of any meaningful recovery. To be kept in this state her minders had to insert a urinary catheter into her bladder and a naso-gastric tube down into her stomach through which she was to be fed and hydrated three times a day with a tasteless nutritious soup.

In the very best of medical institutions where highly trained and skilful surgeons and anaesthetists work with the best of nursing staff and where superb ancilliary help is available these things do and will happen. These are the rare but real complications of general anaesthesia. It would be very wrong of me to attempt the proportioning of any blame to anyone in this awful case. Any doctor, even the very best and kindest of them can find themselves in a situation where someone they are trying to help takes a turn for the worse and is left, by complications of treatments, much worse off than they were pre-treatment. Most of us have found ourselves in that situation at least once in a long, active, professional life. It is very much a case of 'there but for the grace of God go I' and I do not wish to be seen as smug or as pointing the finger at anyone. But I have talked at length to the mother of this young woman and it is clear from my conversations with her that the real problem lay, not so much in the awful tragedy itself, but rather in the lack of any meaningful communications between carers and relatives.

I am not suggesting for one minute that the management of near PVS is simple and straightforward because it is no such thing. Diagnosis can never be absolute and prognosis is always fraught and uncertain. People have been in these states for several years and been known to recover at least partially. But today we know that the relatives of the person in a PVS simply have to be brought into the equation. In as far as possible an explanation should be given as to why it happened and what, if anything, went wrong. There must be no attempt at a cover-up or of anything that might be construed as a cover-up. In addition to this the relatives must be involved in a management strategy and in the decision-making as to how long treatment should go on and to what lengths they should go to keep the sufferer alive. But in this case none of this happened. The young woman's parents were kept in the dark and excluded from all decision-making.

On several occasions the patient developed urinary tract infections as a result of her having to have an in-dwelling catheter. Each of these was treated with antibiotics without discussing it with the family. After twenty years it was decided to insert a gastrostomy feeding tube under general anaesthetic. This was done without discussion with the family. This tube fell out on two occasions and was replaced again without reference to the family. But what was worst of all is that on no occasion were the parents and siblings of the young woman brought into a room and sat down and allowed to express their concerns and to be given a chance to have an input into an overall treatment plan that might envisage eventual closure. That simply never happened. The carers' only plan was to keep the patient alive for as long as ever possible. They claimed to have had an ethical duty to do so.

The family eventually felt that they had no option but to seek legal advice. The first thing they were advised to do was to make the young lady a ward of court. As a ward of court her future would be decided, not by the carers anymore, nor by the family but by the courts of the land. Or, in other words, the courts would stand *in loco parentis* and decide what was the best line of action, what was in the patient's best interests – to go on being fed and hydrated through the artificial means of a gastrostomy tube or to allow for the discontinuation of this method of forced feeding and allow the patient to die? The request to make the patient a ward of court was granted in 1994. From here on in, during court hearings, she was to be referred to simply as 'the ward'.

The next High Court hearing was held in-camera during May 1995 and on 10 May Justice Lynch delivered his verdict, the essence of which was as follows:

- Allow for the discontinuation of feeding via the gastrostomy or naso-gastric tube.
- Allow for the non-treatment of infections and other pathological condition save where pain relief might be required.
- Authorise the family to move the ward to another institution where withholding nutrition was not held to be unethical.

But the carers and the institution where the ward was being cared for decided to appeal this High Court decision to the Supreme Court. On 27 July the Supreme Court delivered its verdict which was essentially to uphold the High Court decision from earlier that summer. I attended all of this hearing as a medical journalist with the *Irish Medical News* and it was at this stage that I first became aware of the family and the long tortuous journey that they had all made over the previous twenty-three painful years. And it wasn't over yet.

After all of this, having had to watch their precious daughter or sister suffer on needlessly for twenty-three long and agonising years at the hands of well-meaning if somewhat blinkered carers, having made her a ward of court and then going through the distress of a High Court hearing followed by an equally stressful Supreme Court hearing, after all of this they were still not out of the woods. No, now they could not find an institution that would take on the case and carry out the legal discontinuation of the tube feeding. Nobody wanted to know about it. It was at this stage that the ward's mother, to know if I might be able to help through my good offices at Clane General Hospital, approached me.

To be honest I did not want to ask my colleagues in Clane Hospital to do something that they may not have been comfortable with or to put them in a position where they may have had to say no. In any case at this stage both the family and I were coming to the same conclusion. The only way and the kindest way forwards was to bring the patient back to her own home where I was to remove the gastrostomy tube and allow her to die surrounded by her loving family. And that's what happened but it wasn't before there was to be a final glitch, this time emanating from the Medical Council.

This whole right to die case attracted huge media attention as you can imagine. In the immediate aftermath of the Supreme Court ruling journalists approached some of the more conservative members of the council's 'fitness to practice' committee. At least one of them, speaking I think to be fair about it on his own behalf, opined that any doctor who would co-operate in the discontinuation of nutritional support for the ward might be deemed guilty of serious professional misconduct and be struck off the register. But I had to balance these kinds of threatening rumbles coming from high quarters with the facts on the ground as I saw them at the time. Those facts were that here was a mother and family who had suffered twenty-three years of the most terrible anguish and pain imaginable, largely at the hands of the medical profession. Now the highest court in the land had at last declared it legal to bring closure and peace and an end to their suffering. If there was anything I could do to help them then I felt duty bound to do so.

Three days after I deflated the retaining balloon and with shaking hand withdrew the gastrostomy feeding tube from deep inside the comatose woman's abdomen, she passed away peacefully and quietly, surrounded by her family and those fantastic nurses who lovingly and so professionally cared for her during her final hours. May she rest in peace.

* * *

My children are now adults living independent lives away from home while Joan and I happily rattle around in this hopelessly impractical old Georgian house. I have sold my general practice to younger blood. At this stage vasectomy has become more or less a full-time job and I certainly do not need the stress and hassle of GP work anymore. People are congratulating me on my 'retirement' and I am at pains to point out that, just because I have given up general practice, this does not at all mean that I have retired. In fact I do not believe in or like the concept of retirement and believe that a man needs to have a good reason to get out of bed every morning. It's either work or wilt and I'd prefer to work. So when well-meaning people congratulate me while mistakenly thinking that I had gone and done something that, as it happens, I do not believe in, they are in effect being mildly offensive – without meaning to be of course.

During the twenty-five years that I served in it, general practice underwent some massive changes. It became a speciality in its own right requiring aspirants to undertake a three-year post-graduate course ending with a membership examination. We are all members of the Irish College of General Practitioners, and sport MICGP after our names. In addition to this general practitioners these days tend to practise within group practices and single-handed practices have now become the exception. This is the very opposite to the way that things were when I set up practice in Kildare on my return from Canada in 1974. Then, single-handed practices were the norm, co-operation among GPs was at best very poor and competition for private patients quite fierce.

Now it is all sweetness and light. Every county has its own GP co-op – an arrangement whereby doctors in any given area cover for each other at nights and weekends. This should add enormously to the quality of general practitioners' personal lives because they can now go to bed at night and know that they are going to get a decent night's sleep. They can go away at weekends or take their children to the beach or climb a mountain and do all these things without the worry that one of their patients may need medical attention in their absence. They are no longer nailed to their practices as we were ten or fifteen years ago. In the bad old days I would be dragged out of my warm winter bed night after night to attend to an asthmatic child or to an old lady who had fallen out of bed or to a couple who had decided to have a good old domestic barney with lots of drink on board too, of course. And the next day I was expected to be fresh and well and all smiles and sympathy throughout a busy day's surgery. And this might go on week in week out for anything up to six months without a break.

That style of general practice is dead and buried and good riddance to it. I say the new order of things, the co-ops, the group practice, the absence of any real competition for private patients, should add enormously to the quality of a GP's personal life. But somehow or other this does not seem to have happened. Other extraneous changes have taken place in the meantime that have negated the internal improvements made in the organisation of community general practices.

The first five years of the new millennium have witnessed quite extraordinary growth and development in the Irish economy and infrastructure. We now have full employment but house prices and mortgages are so high that both parents have to work in order to pay for their lifestyles. They put their infants into crèches and feel guilty about it. They bring their babies to the doctor, not because there is anything wrong with their baby but because they want to assuage their guilt for leaving him or her in a crèche all week. They are assertive, stressed, rude, litigious and computer-literate. People who have done a full internet search before coming to see their GP offer a new challenge. The doctor–patient relationship has changed for all time. The authority of, and respect for, medicine have both gone out the window. Now doctors are on their guard all the time and practising defensive medicine, doing unnecessary laboratory tests just to cover them in the event of litigation. And on top of all that the health services are in such a shambles that it is extremely difficult to get the genuinely sick and urgent cases seen to within a chaotic hospital system.

Such are the stresses and strains and lack of job satisfaction within general practice these days that new recruits to the discipline are hard to find, general practitioners are retiring earlier and there is now a manpower crisis looming in general practice. This is reflected in the fact that many practices have a two or three-day waiting list of patients for non-urgent cases. In my day we didn't even have an appointment system never mind a waiting list of people wanting to come and see you. Changed times indeed from when not so long ago general practitioners would be fighting with each other for stealing 'my patients away from me'!

Clane General Hospital, now in its twentieth year of existence, goes from strength to strength. Even the long-suffering shareholders are happy campers these days because they are in receipt of modest but real annual dividends. A four-million euro extension has just been added to house an MRI and CT scanner along with the many new medical and surgical consultants who have joined us in the recent past. We have an assisted-fertility clinic or IVF unit that is one of the busiest in the country and knee and hip joint replacement surgery has now also been introduced. This is for us a quantum leap forward and brings the whole profile of Clane Hospital up several notches. The place is now vibrant, complete and self-sufficient and I am very proud to have been part of it all through the years. For me at any rate it has gone from a dream, when I first conceived the idea, to a nightmare when we struggled so painfully to survive those dreadful early years wondering where our next penny might come from and how long would it be before the banks foreclosed on us. Then it went back to a dream again when we turned the corner and the whole concept became sustainable, cheerful and even profitable.

* * *

I have taken a keen interest in the subject of 'andropause' or more properly the testosterone deficiency syndrome. All men as they grow older lose their high youthful testosterone levels at a rate of about one per cent per annum. This steady age-related decline in testosterone levels means that by the time a man reaches the age of say seventy or seventy-five he can expect that his testosterone levels will have fallen to less than half of what they were when he was a young man of twenty-one. The question then is this: does this steady natural age-related decline in male hormone levels have any adverse effects on the ageing man and, if it has, is it safe and effective to treat this decline with testosterone replacement therapy? The medical profession is divided on these questions. At the moment there are at least three schools of thought and more research will need to be undertaken before definitive answers can be reached.

The conservative doctors will say that by and large there are no ill effects to this decline in male hormones and even if there were it would be most unsafe to treat them. The majority of medics would I think acknowledge that falling testosterone levels is accompanied by some symptomatology but that this was not worth treating or the potential risks of treating with HRT were such as to make this treatment unwise. And then of course there are the more liberal of us who say that in a minority of men this decline in testosterone levels can produce quality-of-life-reducing symptoms and that in these cases hormone replacement therapy for men is not only justifiable but may also indeed be good medical practice. Opinion is as diverse as that. It has more to do with belief systems than with hard medical facts.

In the meantime however, because I deal with them on a daily basis, I am strongly of the opinion that at least some men do suffer from the consequences of age-related falling testosterone levels and that some of these adverse effects may be reversed by the application of testosterone replacement therapy. Symptoms most commonly encountered are:

- Loss of libido or sex drive
- Erectile dysfunction or impotence
- Increased belly fat and loss of muscle mass and strength
- Lethargy and mild depression
- Osteoporosis and easily fractured bones
- Senile dementia and arteriosclerosis – coronary artery disease.

Before a man can be considered as a candidate for hormone replacement it is essential that his prostate gland be checked for early cancer. This is best done by a blood test known as PSA. Once this is in order it is safe to give him a trial of testosterone replacement. These days this is best given as an intermusclear long-acting injection called Nebido and given every twelve weeks. If after say three of these the man notices no difference at all then therapy should be discontinued. If, as is more likely the case, the man feels better all round then therapy may be continued while keeping an eye on his PSA.

* * *

I am taking a legal action against the state for deliberately poisoning my drinking water. Ever since 1965, when the Health (Fluoridation of Water Supplies) Act 1960 came into law, all public drinking water supplies in Ireland have been fluoridated at a rate of one part per million of fluoride to water. Every county council right across the country is duty bound to add in this fluoride at source, that is at their water treatment plants. They are statutory-bound to do this whether they like it or not and a recent survey indicated that many of them do not like it one little bit and, given the option, they would prefer to discontinue the practice. But they have no option; the law says that they must add in the fluoride to the nation's drinking water supply.

Another statutory body called the Irish Medicines Board defines a medicine as 'any product given to treat, or prevent or diagnose a disease'. Fluoride is given to the Irish population to supposedly prevent or reduce the incidence of a disease called dental caries or tooth decay. Therefore, according to the Irish Medicines Board's own definition of a medicinal product, fluoride is a medicine. Since another duty of the board is to regulate the granting of product authorisation for medicinal products and since fluoride carries no such product authorisation, fluoride is therefore not only a medicine but also, worse still, it is an unlicensed medicine.

By the Department of Health putting this fluoride into Irish drinking water supplies, the population is being mass medicated with an unlicensed medicine. Since we all need our tap water to make a cup of tea or coffee or to water our whiskey then we cannot escape this mass medication and must consume it whether we like it or not. My objection to this practice is not that fluoride probably has no effect on dental caries. I really do not care whether it works or not. Nor am I objecting to it on the basis that this fluoride may be doing me some harm. That doesn't matter all that much either. My objection to this odious practice is that it strips me of my God-given right to make a choice in this aspect of my personal health and is a clear violation of human rights.

Under article 40.3 of the Irish constitution you and I are given a right to bodily integrity. It is my contention, and this may be the linchpin of my upcoming action against the state, that through the non-consensual incursion by the state of a substance into my body, a violation of my constitutional right to bodily integrity has occurred and therefore the Health (Fluoridation of Water Supplies) Act 1960 is unconstitutional and must be struck out.

I know that this has been tried before and failed. The problem, if you like, with our having certain constitutional rights is that the scope and extent of these rights is open to interpretation by our judiciary. That interpretation and analysis may therefore be clouded or rendered biased depending on the prejudices of the individual judge making it. For example back in 1963 a brave young Dublin mother, Gladys Ryan, tried to stop the government from introducing the Health (Fluoridation of Water) Act 1960 by claiming that it would be a violation of her constitutional rights to bodily integrity and to privacy among other things. In other words she took the self same action as I am now undertaking. The Kenny judgement in the Gladys Ryan case interpreted her right to 'bodily integrity' as meaning her right not to undergo any mutilation against her will of body or limb. Or in other words Justice Kenny took an exceedingly narrow and extreme view as to the meaning of bodily integrity – mutilation. Why he took this view may have had something to do with his unwillingness to face down the government of the day. I simply do not know.

Be that as it may however, in the forty-two intervening years things have moved on quite a bit. For example we now have the government's own definition of a medicinal product and fluoridated water would seem to come within that definition. In addition to this, constitutional right to bodily integrity has now been extended by judicial precedent to mean, for example, a right not to have physical contact to which one has not consented. I am not a lawyer of course but it would seem to me that if bodily integrity now extends to physical contact without consent, it should also surely extend to no non-consensual incursion of a substance into the body – no enforced medication against a citizen's will.

In addition to this, in the ward's right to die case in 1996, the Supreme Court ruled that our constitutional right to privacy meant that we had a right to refuse medical treatment even if such a refusal should lead to our death. If it can be shown therefore that fluoridated drinking water is a medicinal product – an inescapable truism in my view, then we already have Irish Supreme Court precedence as to the unconstitutionality of a practice where the right to refuse such medication is denied.

But should my legal challenge to the Irish Health (Fluoridation of Water Supplies) Act 1960 fail in both the Irish High Court and in our Supreme Courts then it should be possible to seek a remedy through the European Court of Human Rights who have a very similar definition to 'medicinal products' as we have in Ireland. Article 5 of the European Convention for the Protection of Human Rights makes it very clear that: 'No one may in principle be forced to undergo an intervention without his or her consent.' In the text of the convention 'intervention' is understood in its widest sense and covers all medical acts including the act of medicating. One way or the other it is my intention to take this matter all the way because otherwise, judging by such government posturing as the recently concluded forum on Fluoridation, paid for by the taxpayer of course, there will never be any change to the status quo. As a blow for civil liberty and human rights this may well be my swan song.

CHAPTER 12

Full Circle

When the gunman left, having fired six times at me at close range and only managing to hit me once, he crossed the road from the surgery and sat down in the middle of a field surrounded by cattle looking at him with his still loaded rifle held across his knees. And the garda brought him out a pint of Guinness. Years later the publican who gave the garda that pint laughingly told me that he is still waiting to be paid for it. And hundreds of people who would have been on their way home from work stopped and got out of their cars to have a look at the scene being played out before them. At this stage I was in an ambulance. Ambulances generally drive too fast and make far too much noise. As a medical insider I can tell you that most of that blue light flashing and sirens blowing is exaggerating the degree of emergency being carried along within. I know it was so in my case. There was a bullet in my right hip joint for God's sake, that's not an emergency.

The late Pope John Paul and I would not have a great deal in common I suspect. But one thing that we do have in common is that we were both shot and we both went in to see our tormentors in prison later. I imagine that we both did that for the same reason – to show ourselves to our would-be assassins as ordinary flesh and blood human beings, to forgive and to bring closure. My man pleaded insanity and was sent to a hospital prison in Dundrum, county Dublin that used to be called the Central Mental Lunatic Asylum. In this day of political correctness this institution is more kindly named today as the Central Mental Hospital. When he had been locked up in there for about three months I asked if I might be allowed to go in and visit him in that grimmest of places. Permission was readily granted.

The Central Mental Hospital was built in 1850 and originally housed eighty men and forty women. Today it has a bed complement of eighty-eight male beds only. It would appear that Irish women no longer need these kinds of facilities. It's men only who become insane, commit a crime and need to be locked away for their own protection. The hospital sits on a thirty-five acre site surrounded by an eighteen-foot high perimeter wall. It is located in a prime residential district of south county Dublin and must be worth an absolute fortune. It is an anachronistic institution of very dubious value reflecting as it does the thinking about mental illness and criminality in the dark ages of medicine.

One enters this dour Victorian pile though high and massive locked gate. Once inside there is a fifty-yard walk up to the hospital-prison itself. The grounds are well maintained by the inmate patients and the place smells of wallflowers. I do not know what this man is doing in here nor what it was that possessed him to come down to Clane and shoot me. But of this I am quite sure – when he pulled the trigger and shot me in the right hip and when he fired at me several times again and, fortunately for me, kept missing, he may have been all fired up, he had had a good few drinks, he may have been very annoyed with me but he was not insane and he should not be locked up in this quasi prison hospital. The place is all locks and keys and bars and chains. It is like a cross between a dog pound and a nursing home. I am shown into this cell-like room where I await my fate.

In due course there is more clattering and banging of gates and bars and big keys engaging with tumblers and my man is shown in and sat down opposite me across a table. We shake hands – all is courteous and calm. He explained to me that eight years ago I had vasectomised him and that shortly following this he developed significant pain and discomfort and that when he brought this to my attention I seemed not to care. Then, on top of that, his wife left him and ran away with another man and his life seemed ruined and it was mostly all my fault. And he then began to build up resentment against me and planned that some day he would shoot me but not kill me. He now felt very sorry and hoped that I could find forgiveness for what he had done to me and to my family.

Forgiveness came easily. I know I am not perfect and at times I can be abrupt. And if he thought that I did not give him the attention he deserved when he developed his post-operative pain then maybe he had a point. Of course this does not excuse his shooting me. Nor does it, even more importantly, excuse his firing at me recklessly five times after hitting me with the first shot. But never mind. The important thing in life is to resolve conflicts and get on with it and this we did. We shook hands again and he remained on in this prison hospital for another two years after which time he was released back into free Ireland. He wrote to me subsequently and apologised again and I consider the matter closed and behind us all.

When, five days post-shooting, Seán Leyden was driving me back to Clane General Hospital after my operation in St James' as we passed the surgery wherein I had been shot I got this incredible urge to go inside into the room where it had all happened. This was not some sort of a whim; it was more an imperative or a compulsion. It was as if some force inside me was saying go in there and take a good look around and that will help you reach some resolution. And I did and it did.

* * *

One mile as the crow flies heading northwest straight out from the front door of Downings House there is a 500-acre wilderness of what we call high-bog, which is bog that has not been cut or otherwise interfered with. Around the periphery of this high-bog there are rougher areas of cutaway-bog, full of drains and ditches and haphazardly naturally planted hazel, ash and birch interspersed with massive informal plantations of gorse, rhododendron and heather. This is where over the centuries turf has been cut away and saved and taken home to keep cabins warm during the long cold winters.

All of this is prime rough-shooting country. The high-bog holds snipe while the cutaway bog holds woodcock. Both snipe and woodcock are winter migratory birds that fly into Ireland from sub-artic countries. They come in at night on the full moon of October and November. They sleep by day and feed by night by probing their long beaks through cattle pads that attract worms up towards the surface. If it becomes too frosty they have to move on because they cannot probe the ground. They move on to the frost-free coast or go further south to France, Spain or even to the Canaries. Snipe and woodcock are mystical creatures.

As you squish your way across the high-bog snipe will rise up in front of you with their characteristic rasping cry of alarm. Some will rise away out of range while others will get up at your feet. It depends to some extent on what way the wind is blowing, on the time of day and how deeply the birds are sleeping. You do not have to have a dog for snipe-shooting other than to help you retrieve a bird that may have been downed in heavy cover. In this situation a good retrieving dog is essential. Otherwise dogs must be restrained on leads and not allowed beat forwards or they will put up too many wild snipe out of range.

When a snipe gets up off the high-bog he grabs the air with his strong broad wings and moves from zero to forty miles an hour in just over two seconds. This bird's acceleration is superior to any other bird or animal that I know of. Because of the way he is grabbing at the air this makes him fly with a zigzag pattern. The whole secret about successful snipe-shooting is to be alert and quick. You move across the bog slowly with the gun held out in front ready to shoot at any second and without warning. You only have a split second to get onto your target. You keep the gun moving at all times and pull the trigger immediately you are above the bird and in the area where you have worked out your snipe will be by the time the shot gets out to him. Shooting does not get much more difficult than this.

Woodcock are distantly related to snipe and offer a different challenge. About twice the size of a snipe they generally favour warm and waterproof places of shelter. Under holly trees or rhododendron bushes or in the bracken on the sunny slopes of evergreen forests, those are the haunts favoured by this silent bird. You must have a dog or dogs with you when you go woodcock shooting, otherwise you are, as they say, at nothing. Woodcock will lie there and not make a move unless forced to do so by a springer spaniel. That is how these dogs get their name – they spring game. Cocker spaniels take their name from woodcock shooting. Just like snipe when woodcock are on the wing, they are fast and elusive.

These days, while far from being a wealthy man, I can afford some things that were out of the question when the children were growing up. One such indulgence is driven shooting. Of all the various forms of game shooting this is the most formal and ordered. It is also, of course, the most expensive. Derived from Victorian times when the modern shotgun was invented, driven shoots are usually held on large private estates of several hundred acres where pheasants and partridge and maybe mallard are raised on the estate specifically for the shoot which typically will be held every second weekend throughout the shooting season.

On the day of the shoot there will be eight or ten guns. Sometimes the guns 'share' with the two shooters, shooting every second drive. There will be five drives on any given day, three before lunch and two afterwards. The shoot manager who is bound by law to start the day off with a short lecture on gun safety oversees the guns. After the lecture lots are drawn for pegs. If you draw for example number two then you will be on peg number two for the first drive, number four for the second drive and so on up like that. In any given drive, even on the best and most expensive shoots, there will be times when no birds at all will come over certain pegs and the gun standing there will fire no shots at all. It is really a matter of luck how you are drawn on any given day. Generally you will have good drives and not so good ones. The manager takes out the guns to the first drive, usually sitting on bales of straw on the back of a tractor-trailer, and places them at their peg. On the trailer also will be some dogs and their handlers. The shotguns are kept in 'sleeves' at all times until you are at your peg. The pegs are back some thirty yards from the wood, forest or thicket from which the birds are to be driven.

There will be up to twenty 'beaters', mostly young people earning a few extra bob and also having a good day out. Some beaters will have dogs with them; mostly young springers are used. Others, armed with long sticks, are called 'stoppers' and these people keep to the outside of the drive and stop birds running out the sides. They tap the trees with their sticks or flap plastic flags noisily to keep the birds in. The gamekeeper usually oversees the beaters and determines how fast or slowly they move through the cover. A good drive is where the birds get up in ones and twos. A bad drive is where the birds get up in big bunches and the drive is over in a few minutes. Dribbling the birds out in small groups takes considerable skill and is what earns the keeper a good tip at the end of the day. The drive is started with the sounding of a hunting horn at a time when everyone is in place: guns, beaters and 'picker uppers' with their retrievers. This time is agreed between shoot manager and head gamekeeper communicating with each other over walkie-talkies.

Now the shooting starts and the place comes alive with the roar of shotguns. The 'guns' wear earplugs or earmuffs. During the lecture earlier the guns have been warned to keep their barrels pointing skywards while waiting for the driven birds to come their way. Also they will have been told not to shoot at any 'low birds' or ground game; a low bird is one that does not have plenty of clear sky all around it. Shooting at low birds endangers the beaters coming through the woods. A gun who repeatedly offends in this manner may be asked to go home or more likely asked not to come back to that shoot again. Safety is always a big issue at these shoots and rightly so. Every year beaters get injured in Ireland, mostly only slightly but sometimes badly enough to lose the sight in one eye.

After the first drive the beaters move on to the next thicket or wood while the dog-men put their labradors and springers to work picking up. The guns pick up their empty cartridges, sleeve up their shotguns and move back to the tractor-trailer. At this stage maybe sloe gin is passed around and everyone wants to know how the other got on. A fine day on a shoot like this is very sociable, relaxing and good fun. A wet cold winter's day is a different story of course. But even then there is always the few drinks and a few songs or tunes on the whistle back in the hotel afterwards.

This life is short and so we ought to try and make it merry.
When things look dreary then take good cheer in fine old port and sherry.
Though some they may choose another muse old Bacchus wins I'm thinking
And in cellar cool I'll take a stool and start drinking, drinking, and drinking.